I0031194

Applications of Accounting Information Systems

Applications of Accounting Information Systems

David M. Shapiro

BEP BUSINESS EXPERT PRESS

Applications of Accounting Information Systems
Copyright © Business Expert Press, LLC, 2020.

All rights reserved. No part of this publication may be reproduced, stored in a retrieval system, or transmitted in any form or by any means—electronic, mechanical, photocopy, recording, or any other except for brief quotations, not to exceed 250 words, without the prior permission of the publisher.

First published in 2020 by
Business Expert Press, LLC
222 East 46th Street, New York, NY 10017
www.businessexpertpress.com

ISBN-13: 978-1-94999-158-1 (paperback)
ISBN-13: 978-1-94999-159-8 (e-book)

Business Expert Press Financial Accounting, Auditing, and Taxation Collection

Collection ISSN: 2151-2795 (print)
Collection ISSN: 2151-2817 (electronic)

Cover image licensed by Ingram Image, StockPhotoSecrets.com
Cover and interior design by S4Carlisle Publishing Services Private Ltd., Chennai, India

First edition: 2020

10 9 8 7 6 5 4 3 2 1

Printed in the United States of America.

Abstract

The revolutionary effects of using accounting information systems by displacing manual information systems in the private and public sectors cannot be overstated. The benefits of this substitution of set of processes include increased mathematical accuracy, predefined fields and coding tasks, and de-emphasis of manual clerical labor in favor of labor adept in data processing.

Reporting can be significantly automated, facilitating managerial power and control at a distance and the proliferation of global enterprises. The potential detriments are rarely accurately, completely, and timely addressed as information system vendors, management consultants, and corporate procurement teams race toward the popularly conceived state of the art. Systems are ballyhooed as continually improving in processing speed, functionality, and capacity.

Users of these automated systems may not consider big picture effects, and they may not intelligently consider the conduct risks to their own enterprises by concentrating such global reach and influence at high levels of senior management without dedicating adequate resources to verifying the accuracy, completeness, and timeliness of the information systems. This book considers these risks.

Keywords

risk assessment; transaction cycle; risk mitigation; fraud detection; information risk; automated system; oversight; preventive control; detective control; internal audit.

Contents

Acknowledgments

While I acknowledge the invaluable assistance I've received in my professional life at institutions such as Kroll Associates, where so many talented individuals took the time and care to educate me on the uses and abuses of computer-based systems, and in my academic life at the John Jay College of Criminal Justice, where I am still learning how to think and express myself carefully and intelligently, I would likely not have written more than a word or two without the encouragement of Ed Stone, a man whose guidance is gentle and practical. Mr. Stone, whom I've gotten to know over the years through social media and e-mails, is a better teacher than I am. He is detail oriented and never misses a holiday greeting. I am lucky to have benefited from his inspection and oversight of my writing plans. He's smart, humble, and wise enough to vacation in New England in the summers.

Also, *salud* to my family: Susan (the spouse), Emily Rose (the daughter), and Ari B. (the son). There's more: Otos and Ephialtes—the adopted cats. This group is collectively chaotic (can't remember when we all agreed on anything material) and individually courageous (no need to remind them of the value of independence). Again, I am lucky to be associated with these individuals.

That, of course, is the scariest part: Luck has brought me serendipity, and life gets no better than this.

PART A

Executive Summary of Accounting Information Systems

This book comprises Part A (including an executive summary) and Part B of a five-part series. Part B discusses and analyzes accounting information systems (AISs) through an introductory chapter; a chapter on enterprise AISs; a chapter on e-business AISs; a chapter on health care industry AISs; and a chapter on internal controls relevant to AISs. Part B is intended as both a survey and a prompt to discover further ideas germane to the changing technology and social approaches to using, managing, and negotiating through the networks of AISs affecting many of us, especially those of us in the United States.

The ideas in this book serve as a theoretical and conceptual foundation to further discussion and research about the strengths, weaknesses, opportunities, and threats presented by the modern era's movement away from manual recordkeeping and report writing to computer-based records and reports. While authoritative literature has been reviewed in the preparation of this book, it is not intended to provide a systematic and comprehensive review and summary of the literature. The book is perhaps better approached as a critical thinker's introduction to potential and actual effects of high dependency on AISs to govern and manage organizations, recognizing that technology's benefits are often widely touted but its risks given less public exposure and examination.

This book is intended neither as a primer on how to use an AIS nor as a quantitative study on the effects of AISs on labor markets at the macro-level or specific effects at particular organizations (i.e., the meso level). That organizations conduct thorough cost–benefit analyses before committing to expensive and long-term investments in an AIS infrastructure speaks for itself. Moreover, these costs include making the infrastructure environment user-friendly—a specification that typically demands both a short period of user and supervisor training and a short period of repetitive practice by the users within the AIS environment.

Indisputably, organizations have moved to AIS environments, and the consensus would deem this progress. Small, medium, and large organizations rely heavily on computer-based accounting and auditing; this is accepted as a given in this book. Also, I accept that globalization, including offshoring of administrative and other necessary organizational functions, would be significantly impaired without the advantages provided through computer-based AISs.

However, I discuss displacement effects as required occupational skills shift from knowledge-intensive public accounting skills to technological know-how in hardening and softening AISs (i.e., customizing) for the particular user environment. This shifting in employer demand results from exploiting the advantages of the AIS environment (primarily, low- to medium-skilled clerks) over the disadvantages of the non-AIS environment (primarily, extensive processing and reporting with the assistance of high-skilled public accountants). Generally, costs to the employer are directly related to the skill level required of the laborer, other things being equal.

Of course, it is possible that computer-based AISs reduce the overall required quantity of clerical labor and increase the demand for and quality of high-skilled labor such as public accountants, though this condition would tend to threaten and lessen the advantages of offshoring to jurisdictions considered less developed and populated with cheaper laborers. However, any assumption that high tech is an across-the-board and win–win benefit for all should be carefully reconsidered (Hao 2019).

Together, Parts A and B do not create a consumers' guide to AIS procurement. They will serve to alert the careful reader that while AIS presents advantages of efficiency, it also burdens us with risks that may not be adequately disclosed elsewhere. *Caveat emptor* cannot be overemphasized. Leaders, management, and other decision and policy makers should develop near-term and long-term perspectives of the effects of concentration of information and human resources management in the algorithms of the machine.

Generally, AISs allow greater depth and breadth to the analysis and practical application of data including the issuance of reports based on the records within the AIS. However, information risk comprises the threats of misinformation (i.e., error) and disinformation (i.e., fraud). The likelihood and severity of these risks may also become enhanced by AISs, given their opacity, complexity, and potential abuse by employees, especially high managerial agents such as those occupying the C-suite (e.g., CEO, chief financial officer [CFO]). Boards of directors and other governance officials should not trust AIS blindly. Mitigation and remediation of these risks demand high levels of external (e.g., public auditors) and internal (e.g., internal audit function) inspection and oversight—manual and automated.

Specifically, via proper training and feedback, AISs require and modify the knowledge and skills used in the operating, financing, and investing functions of the enterprise through the following mechanisms:

- The physical and logical structures of an AIS allow action at a distance, coordination of strategy, and development of relevant financial and nonfinancial data.
- Documentation of the AIS through narratives, flowcharts, and other diagrammatic techniques allows transferability of jobs and tasks among employees and agents, potentially minimizing the risk of loss resulting from departure of key employees.
- Communication of details of transactions in a computerized environment minimizes the risk of loss through casualty, economic sabotage, and so on by facilitating efficient data transfers and effective backup systems.
- Building automated and semiautomated internal controls into the AIS such that general and application controls are hardened into the control environment, minimizing the risk of fraud and error.
- The capture of essential process cycles such as revenues, expenditures/expenses, financing, human resources, production, sales, and customer service by the AIS, assuring that routine transactions are recorded and reported systematically and nonroutine transactions are flagged for further inspection and oversight.

In brief, the study and practice of AIS operation, management, inspection, and oversight enhance the development of critical thinking skills, including the ability to negotiate the following processes and tasks:

- The design, implementation, maintenance, and remediation of a semiautomated system of journals and ledgers;
- The design, implementation, maintenance, and remediation of a semiautomated system of financial and nonfinancial reporting through database management and spreadsheets.

The AIS supports the accounting, auditing, fraud risk, and related programs through its direct enhancement of the compliance function and its enforcement. Data, evidence, and analyses therefrom that raise the issue of potential violation of law, regulation, rule, contract, or code of ethics may be timely detected, prevented, or otherwise deterred through administrative feedback mechanisms, including the inspection and oversight provided through the internal audit function.

Moreover, effective inspection and oversight require access to information and transparency; this is essential for honest insiders and diligent outsiders: "(those) who watch standard signals of market activity to determine their behavior, but who fail to understand that the usual behavior of their signals has been altered by unsuspected looting" (Akerlof et al. 1993, 57). Thus, standard analyses based on traditional metrics may suffer from manipulated disclosures of data, as well as the threat of material omissions, demanding enhanced exploration to mitigate information risk.

There are internal threats (e.g., rogue employees, vulnerable systems), and there are threats arising from cyber-assisted, cyber-dependent, and cyber-enabled crimes that may (or may not) originate externally (Wall 2018, 33). Both of these typologies of wrongdoing may impair the effectiveness of any given AIS. As noted by the FBI, cyber-enabled crimes are on the rise (FBI 2018), including the following bad conduct facilitated through computer-based technology exploiting human and other control environment vulnerabilities not prevented by the AIS and control activities in place:

- Business e-mail compromises, which include e-mails spoofing an authorized officer such as the enterprise's CFO and fraudulently causing wire transfers from the enterprise to an account controlled by the cybercriminal.

- Payroll diversions, which include phishing e-mails used to fraudulently obtain the log-in credentials of employees for the purpose of changing direct deposit account instructions.
- Tech support frauds, which include the fraudulent offering of services to remedy alleged but nonexistent problems in the victim's software applications that result in transfers of funds by the victim to the cybercriminal in pursuit of the bogus solution.
- Extortion, which includes sextortion and other illicit means that threaten to or harm the victim's reputation under threat of disclosure, often accompanied by demands for payment in a virtual currency to avoid detection.

These illustrations of risk inherent in the current era's dependence on computer-based means to conduct business provide public services, process and record transactions such as funds transfers, and communicate key trade secrets such as proprietary analyses, and thus, detailed cost and pricing data and summary reports need to be controlled. However, absolute control would be cost prohibitive. The probabilities and severities of harms should be estimated through enlightened risk assessment procedures and efficient risk mitigation strategies facilitated by AIS data and programs.

Given the risks of false positives (i.e., type I errors) and false negatives (i.e., type II errors), the practical need for efficient problem solving regarding the accuracy, completeness, and timeliness of accounting data production cannot be overestimated. Importantly, theorizing and conceptualizing about AIS is primarily an exercise in uncertainty; that is, we make decisions under conditions of uncertainty and not under conditions of known probabilities, also known as decisions under risk (Hansson 2018). While promoters of AIS capacity and performance are easy to find, detractors may be marginalized under the pejorative term "luddite"; these conflicting activities do not necessarily result in a fair presentation and disclosure of actual performance, quantifiable risk, and uncertain outcomes.

Exhibit A-1 provides a bird's-eye viewpoint of the treatment of issues raised in Part B of this book.

Exhibit A-1

High-level overview of Part B

Part B	Information risk	Conduct risk	Inspection and oversight
Introduction	Falsity of accounting data	Automation facilitates blind compartmentalization	Continuous internal audit realized
Enterprise	Enterprise resource planning (ERP) assumption and estimate rigidity	Excessive high managerial agent discretion	Accountability through comprehensive audit
E-business	Compromised feedback loop	Privacy and confidentiality threatened	Triple bottom-line accounting
Health care	Complex medical and insurance data	Third-party intermediary and payer error and fraud	Systemic monitoring by regulators

The general and application internal controls required to mitigate against information and conduct risk should include a robust computer forensics program routinely embedded in the internal audit function. The practical ability to obtain timely feedback on items such as access by employees and agents, changes to files, deletion of data, and so on should be available. Computer-based data are often as easy to disappear as made apparent in the recordkeeping and reporting. Having such feedback in a format readily useful in court not only supports a valuable control mechanism against rogue or collusive conduct but may also be admitted in courts of law and supportive of investigative and prosecutorial efforts, where necessary (e.g., to remedy damages caused by employees, agents, or others such as hackers). The prospective harms resulting from wrongful transfer of sensitive or confidential data demand no less.

Moreover, due care should be exercised in the design, implementation, and assessment of the AIS. For example, with respect to health care AISs, how does the technology integrate health care concerns such as forward-looking statements of required, expected, or desirable costs to maintain health with billing concerns such as historical statements of accounts receivable with accurate and complete contractual adjustments and so on, if at all? Key inquiries should focus not only on *qui bono* but *qui perdidit*. As an example, hospital patients are too often unpleasantly surprised by their bills meticulously prepared with the aid of AISs that serve to benefit other entities in the health care system without providing the necessary transparency for fairness and full disclosure to these patients (Bluth 2019).

Of course, surprise hospital bills may only be the proverbial tip of the iceberg as the underlying natural complexity to health care issues such as proper treatment for cancer and artificial complicatedness of invoicing and related services facilitated by AISs of health care practitioners and insurance companies tend to create an unmanageable system, especially at the patient level (Silvers 2019). Moreover, effects at the macro (society-wide) level need further consideration as AIS along with other technologies displace workers (Edin et al. 2019).

For clarity in presentation I've broken down Part B's key takeaways into the three questions identified below. While these questions and answers provide helpful summaries of the contents of each chapter within Part B, they should not be interpreted as a complete recitation of the discussion and analysis in the chapters. Careful and critical reading of the entirety of the book is my recommendation, albeit seemingly self-serving.

Key Questions of Part B

1. *What does the five-part series on AIS say about it? (e.g., What is the overall risk assessment, including fraud risk?)*

AISs exist to further the accountability of the individuals responsible for stewardship of an entity's resources, including the disposition of assets. They are an essential tool in creating a responsible control environment, allowing control activities and mitigating risks that might have been unheard of in manual control systems. From providing assurance about the data inputs and processing to monitoring conduct risk through extensive real-time surveillance and feedback techniques, the AIS supports organizational goals of efficiency and effectiveness through its distribution of access to information and transparency in management and inspection and oversight.

Access to information may be distributed globally, allowing breadth of shared decision making. Transparency results from the shared language of accounting and related metrics designed to further the organizational goals and objectives, depending on the accuracy, completeness, and timeliness of reporting of the entity. AISs should be designed, implemented, and maintained to facilitate the goal of accountability and its supporting objectives, with the AIS providing timely feedback about operations. Thus, AISs are not only a key component of the entity's control environment but an essential means to build understanding, morale, trust, and collective action in support of goals and objectives.

However, the AIS also supports increased compartmentalization. The daisy chain of nodes within the network may preclude many from developing a coherent understanding of the organization's activities. Big picture thinking may be reserved only for those atop the hierarchy. As integrity, competency, and objectivity may not be coordinated with ascension in the hierarchy, the organization may suffer from risks attendant to compartmentalization, including group-think, tunnel vision, and go-along to get-along attitudes. Key decision making, whether top-down from the C-suite or small operational committees, is not necessarily enhanced.

While this book does not provide any specific recommendations as to what vendors to use in seeking to acquire, deploy, and maintain an AIS, it provides an assessment of how AISs should be interpreted and monitored by nontechnical individuals providing inspection and oversight of the reporting entity. Reliance on the AIS to satisfy compliance and regulatory requirements is a generally accepted practice. However, regulators may be captured or otherwise ineffective, demanding an independent means of assessing AIS efficacy (e.g., public auditors, internal auditors). Of course, who will timely test the so-called guardians, such as credit rating agencies and public auditors, for the benefit of the organization?

A key question of this book is, what happens when modern AISs displace accounting, auditing, and monitoring by highly skilled professionals with heavy reliance on algorithmic and mechanical means to oversee the entity's performance? Will cost-conscious managers set too high standards against which further investigation is necessary, resulting in too many false negatives? Does the control environment become altered such that a culture presenting an intolerable risk of control fraud and predation of stakeholders, including clients or customers, ensues (i.e., an environment that tends toward the criminogenic) (see Black 2011)? While these issues are not Likely to be resolved one way or the other in general, trust in the machine at the expense of the organic needs recognition and evidence-based assessment, in particular, to weigh properly the attendant risks. The black box may be fast, but it is amoral and subject to managerial manipulation.

Exhibit A-2 identifies a rational approach to estimating the general effects of AIS on the transaction cycle broken down into its component elements.

Exhibit A-2

AIS effects on transaction cycle

Transaction cycle	Strength	Weakness	Opportunity	Threat
Initiation	Institutionally memorialized	Semi- or unstructured data	Robust accountability	Limited auditability
Authorization	Robust audit trail	Unresponsive to improved practice	Consensus at a distance	Side agreement exclusion
Recording	Validity checks on data	Reliability checks curtailed	Blockchain-type hardening	Control through silos
Processing	Efficiency of throughput	Inadequate time to verify	Real-time communication	Black box to audit team
Reporting	Transparent and standardized	Errors in accounting classifications	Global and industry uniformity	Fraudulent exploitation

AISs may result in accurate, complete, and timely reporting. However, they may facilitate compartmentalization such that effective monitoring by internal and public auditors, criminal investigators, regulators and public prosecutors, investors' attorneys, and the media, especially the financial press, whether from inside or outside of the entity, is impaired without compensating controls. AISs may tilt the balance of control under the thumb of potentially unchecked high managerial agent discretion to a level where accountability may be thwarted. For example, while an effective AIS may tend to thwart the risk of bribery, it may not comprise a sufficient means for this objective (see Wu 2005).

Whereas developers and sellers of AISs are available to tout the wonderful and useful processing functions of a given AIS, as well as the enormous input and output and report-writing capacities, the risks inherent in committing to such automation undoubtedly present disclosed and undisclosed harms that are unlikely to have been validly and reliably assessed by independent and impartial experts and scholars. Financial and other incentives, including marketing and promotion plans, greatly favor the deification of modern technology, including computer-based AISs. As usual, *caveat emptor* and *qui bono*?

Lest we forget, "… auditors will focus on what is asked of them" (Simon, Smith, and Zimbelman 2018, 275). If high managerial agents do not demand that fraud risk be assessed and addressed against them, then fraud and other misconduct knowingly or recklessly initiated and/or approved by them may be neither effectively prevented nor timely detected by the monitoring function, notwithstanding the sophistication of the AIS in place.

Computerized AISs have enhanced the functionality of preparing financial statements on a timely basis. Additionally, accuracy and completeness have been improved as internal checks on inputs reduce the risk of data entry errors. Moreover, the computer-based AIS processes transactions and organizes data at speeds that dwarf what can be prepared by manual AISs. These software application tools facilitate both external financial reporting and internal managerial (cost) accounting, including improvements to laying a detailed audit trail and allowing historical data to be retrieved rapidly (Ghasemi et al. 2011). In brief, the capacity for accurate, complete, and timely management of inputs, processing, and outputs is expanded to a level rendering manual AISs obsolete. Nonetheless, there are potentially negative effects.

While AISs have provided several clearly established benefits for organizations, including the capacity to manage and use volumes of data efficiently and timely, there are detriments and risks in every system, whether entirely manual or primarily automated. In a relevant scholarly article on virtual and online domains, Dilla et al. (2013) argue that control systems designed and imposed top-down may lack the degree of commitment to integrity, including antifraud and antitheft practices and procedures, that control systems consensually adapted and voluntarily adopted by a broader base within the organization would exhibit. That is, assets are more effectively protected where a code of integrity is shared rather than crammed down.

I note that having employees and agents electronically sign and swear they've read, understood, and agree to the organization's code of business conduct does not rise to shared values. These codes are often signed with a state of mind similar to that accompanying the acceptance of end-user licensing agreements (EULAs) required in many instances to access and use proprietary software applications through the Internet.

Modern AISs are designed and implemented not only to record and report accurately, completely, and timely but also in compliance with general and specific authorization over the disposition of assets and initiation and processing of transactions. These labor and resource control systems are vetted by experts and purchased at the C-suite level. Rarely would rank and file be allowed meaningful, ex ante input into the decision-making process. Moreover, the labor displacement induced by large-scale AISs may exert a resentful blowback among surviving employees.

As AISs do not operate in a vacuum independent of the specific culture that they serve, and recognizing that serious fraud and error may occur, especially where the likelihood of collusion is increased, the intangible and unpredictable effects of senior management commitment to excessive automation should be profoundly considered. By way of illustration, the infamous fraud committed by the Madoff organization would not likely have occurred without the capacity of an entity-wide AIS concentrating control at the top of the organization (see U.S. Securities and Exchange Commission 2012a).

2. *What are key takeaways (e.g., how do professionals deal with AIS and its strengths and weaknesses)?*

With the trend of capital expenditures focused on increasing efficiency, especially in the acquisition, implementation, and maintenance of AISs, the role of the auditor, whether internal or external, adapts accordingly. The novice auditor may be trained under information technology to act like an expert for the purpose of examining and assessing the representational faithfulness of financial statements without enduring the years of experience often required to become such an expert (Rose et al. 2012). In brief, fraud cues may be embedded in structured computer-based decision aids to accelerate and enhance the performance of even inexperienced auditors.

If the laboratory experiments that formed the bases for the authors' conclusion hold across the high-stakes practitioner environment, the added value of the audit function would be invaluable to counter potentially the trend of deskilling (i.e., displacing accounting and auditing experts with comparatively low-paid clerical labor using expensive computer-based systems) widely resulting from greater reliance on information technology.

Of course, auditors generally provide detective and/or compensating controls and not primarily preventive controls, so the value of training novice auditors using fraud cues in decision aids, while likely helpful in some material respects, is not without limitations.

Other scholarly research focused on the helpfulness of supporting decision making about risk assessment with stories rather than checklists (see Bierstaker et al. 2018). This too was found to aid novices in acting like experts. The development of knowledge structures, illustrating both the nature of fraud and how to discover it, was enhanced with even simple narratives and analysis (i.e., identifying fraud cues on the basis of similarity in effect—correlations between conditions that closely accompany actual fraud) of fraudulent financial reporting. The effective use of novices in lieu of more expensive and less common experts in accounting and auditing would contribute to the value of automated AISs and potentially mitigate against risks of deskilling.

While the literature puts forth intriguing and thought-provoking laboratories of controlled experimentation (usually involving accounting students and so-called experienced auditors of global public accounting firms), these theories and concepts may apply only where the domain of fraud and error is deemed comparatively small. In brief, the actual record of fraud detection, even by experienced auditors, is fairly sparse, suggesting the unsatisfactorily unquantified risk of false negatives among public auditors. An AIS that is not periodically and continuously tested for fraud and error by demonstrably proficient sleuths of fraud detection (cf. potentially bounded external and internal auditors) may result in unsound financial and managerial (internal) reporting of intolerable length.

Exhibit A-3

AIS risk remediation, mitigation, and testing

Key activities	Goals	Risks	Effectiveness measures
Continuous internal auditing	To assure integrity of internal reporting	Cost burden threatens competitiveness	Management by exception reports decrease
Robust external auditing	To assure integrity of AIS inputs, process, and outputs	Price of audit increased with need for highly skilled auditors	Auditor management letter addresses through the box assessment
Robust governance, risk management, and compliance function	To supplement internal audit function with diverse and innovative approach to data management	GRC function does not seek sufficient independent evidence	Integrated routine reporting by affected functions such as internal audit and legal

As noted in Exhibit A-3, key operating and inspection and oversight activities in themselves are not novel. It is the level of commitment to these activities that is the essential mediating variable. Cost centers such as auditing and related governance, risk, and compliance (GRC) functions do not directly return profits. Organizations may tend to lend insufficient support to cost centers to benefit more heavily revenue and investment centers that directly contribute to profitability. For a notorious example of collapse of a large organization in the political economy notwithstanding the long-term presence of a formerly reputable public auditor and rigorous (at least as documented) GRC functions, see the Enron case (U.S. Department of Justice 2014).

Establishment of documentation, a process and output facilitated with computer-based AISs, is not sufficient. Integrity and effectiveness of codes of conduct demand continuous vigilance by internal employees and external agents to increase the probability of successful outcomes; that is, a control environment characterized by compliance with the letter of the law and the spirit of ethical commitment. This goal requires that public auditors and internal compliance and control specialists such as internal auditors perform deep and impartial (not merely independent) analyses of the organization's data (e.g., auditing not only the outputs of the AIS but through the processes and algorithms embedded in computers), whether structured in journals and ledgers or unstructured in e-mails and memoranda.

3. *Where do we stand today? (e.g., how do we prepare ourselves for an expanded and deepened role for AIS and related technology?)*

Practically, "the program user has two options: to record properly economic transactions and operations based on documents issued or received, or the option in which he fails to record or records erroneously those operations, destroying, altering or "extinct" certain documents" (Puiu and Nistor 2013, 5). Thus, the accuracy and completeness of the data entry function is key for assessing program integrity and efficacy, whether for the preparation of general purpose external financial reports or internal special purpose management reports.

At issue is more than the reliability of a given computer-based AIS: accounting may just as readily serve to obscure reality as disclose it with representational faithfulness, and as the stakes are high (e.g., a loss of confidence in the markets and a perceived diminishing of the reliability of the numbers produced through the AIS may lead to significant destruction of capitalized value of the organization), there should be a call not only for technical accuracy, completeness, and timeliness in recording and reporting data but for a commitment to transparency. Loss contingency analyses and other accounting procedures required under generally accepted accounting principles (GAAPs) are required even, if not especially, where the result may be unfavorable for the reporting entity.

Access to reliable information is not only a reporting entity concern but a genuine concern of civil society at large (see Lehman and Okcabol 2005). To the extent that relevant markets and the community at large lose confidence in the public reporting of organizations the society itself is threatened with loss of cohesion and worse. The AIS directly not only serves the reporting entity but also indirectly serves the environment in which the entity operates.

Assessment of the validity and reliability of the AIS demands more than reference to traditional financial metrics (e.g., analytical procedures based entirely on accounting data) and accounting data (e.g., asset and liability valuation). The use of nonfinancial information (e.g. number of employees) should be captured within the AIS as corroborating data and be readily accessible to users, auditors, regulators, and other stakeholders. Access to information interpreted broadly (i.e., accounting data and corroborating data, including nonfinancial data) is essential for effective control activities such as monitoring and fraud risk assessment. Accurate, complete, and timely financial reporting should consider and weigh nonfinancial information (see Brazel, Jones, and Prawitt 2014). This would include unstructured data embedded in e-mails, memoranda, and so on. The temptation to let unstructured data lie may be deemed reckless in a criminogenic or weak control environment.

Computer-based AISs have drastically improved accountability for organizations. However, more can and will be done (see Exhibit A-4).

Exhibit A-4

General forecast of AIS pathways

AIS pathway	Inputs	Processes	Outputs	Outcomes
Near term	Image and voice recognition enhancement	Enhanced fiber-optic processing	GAAP-ready general purpose financial reports	Minimizing lag between private recording and public reporting of transactions
Medium term	Real-time movements translated to accrual accounting	Enhanced wireless processing	Efficacy and integrity internal reporting	Minimizing lag between realization of conduct risk and remediation of error and fraud

While prediction is a fool's game, as indicated in Exhibit A-4, I believe that enhancements in efficiency are virtually inevitable. Hopefully, these will be accompanied by rising levels of integrity in AIS performance at the hardware, software, and user levels. Perhaps, the holy grail of effectiveness may be approached: conflicts of interest often plague the customer and investor. Where there are side agreements not fully and fairly disclosed to the decision makers of the organization, dispositions of assets and other transactions affecting outside parties' rights and obligations may be unduly influenced and perhaps reach the level of fraud.

Perhaps one day an AIS fully integrated with relevant outside sources of information may empower quick, reliable, and enhanced due diligence such that the organization and its investors and customers are treated consistent with their bargained-for rights, with related party transactions adequately disclosed and controlled for commercial reasonableness.

Discussion and Analysis

Currently, AIS performance evaluation may be aided by reference to standards developed by the following bodies (not intended as an exhaustive list):

- ISACA's (formerly known as the Information Systems Audit and Control Association) COBIT (Control Objectives for Information and Related Technologies) frameworks and research;
- ISO's (International Organization for Standardization) standards and research, including risk management and management system standards;
- NIST's (National Institute of Standards and Technology) information technology and cybersecurity;
- Axelos's ITIL (Information Technology Infrastructure Library).

Other organizations offer training or certificate programs including the following (without limitation or endorsement):

- AICPA's (American Institute of Certified Public Accountants) information management and assurance certificates (AICPA 2019);
- CIMA's (Chartered Institute of Management Accountants) qualifications framework;
- IMA's (Institute of Management Accountants) certificate in management accounting (CMA) program.

General and application controls would be tested and audited per COSO (Committee of Sponsoring Organizations of the Treadway Commission) guidance (COSO 2019) and PCAOB (Public Company Accounting Oversight Board) standards, where applicable.

Importantly, implementation of information technology may lower costs and improve organizational performance (U.S. Government Accountability Office 2019; see also U.S. Government Accountability Office 2010). Mechanisms such as shared services, data standardization, and streamlining of services through elimination of duplicative or redundant services improve performance by reducing costs and quickening service delivery.

Case studies demonstrate that enterprise resource planning AISs facilitate continuous auditing, thereby increasing transparency of the data and processes, making audits more efficient, and potentially exposing corporate fraud (see Haynes and Li 2016). Nonetheless, other studies demonstrate contrary results with respect to fraud risk assessment. For example, a study of 72 audit seniors and four audit managers from a Big 4 firm indicated that they did not accurately assess fraud risk derived from known fraudulent financial reporting using computer-based technology designed to decompose and facilitate risk assessment (see Mock, Srivastava, and Wright 2017).

Generally, novice and experienced auditors (and accountants) have little professional experience with fraud, even those working at Big 4 firms. The type II risk (i.e., false negatives) may be substantial and unquantifiable based on current approaches. This is understandable where one accepts the idea that AISs are not designed specifically to detect fraud; instead, they are tools to facilitate data entry, processing, and report writing. Garbage-in, garbage-out (GIGO) is not prevented. Overall, the use of information and communications technology, including AISs, may contribute to both integrity and efficacy in the entity's operations and reporting (see Bhattacherjee and Shrivastava 2018).

Notwithstanding the difficulties inherent in fraud detection, especially as methods of commission and concealment vary across entities and industries, there seems little doubt that expert audit systems may be adapted to enhance the fraud risk assessment of inexperienced auditors. See Lombardi and Dull (2016) for a study in the implementation of such a technological decision aid in the health care field. In fact, the use of AISs allows for other data such as process logs to supplement the evidence and resolve fraud risk issues (Baader and Krcmar 2018). See also Nissan (2013) for a discussion and analysis of data mining, including link and text analyses, to identify, explore, and prove the activities and nature of criminal networks and detect fraud at the individual and entity levels.

Nonetheless, the use of human intelligence such as focused and adaptive interviews to supplement the AIS in resolving fraud and conduct risk issues may not be circumvented and avoided any time soon (see Warren and Schweitzer 2018).

However, some questions remain unanswered:

- How do we translate fraud risk assessment into fraud detection? The use of historical case studies taken from sources such as the U.S. Securities and Exchange Commission (SEC) Accounting and Enforcement Releases (U.S. Securities and Exchange Commission 2012b) may not predict future frauds. Moreover, some details may be omitted from the SEC civil and administrative investigations, whether or not resulting in criminal referrals and investigations by the FBI.
- How do we interpret and generalize expert knowledge, declarative and procedural, as espoused by senior audit staff? These individuals may or may not have adequate broad-based experience with actual fraud investigations. Moreover, even having been an expert in a given case (e.g., Enron) may not support the valid and reliable presence of a skill in fraud detection widely.
- How do we evaluate the efficacy of specific algorithms, whether designed to develop fraud risk assessment or to detect fraud in fact, where these are proprietary and unavailable to the researchers (as in the Lombardi and Dull article noted earlier)? That an expert system can be developed to show that a historical fraud did evince factors of high risk of fraud may not prove enough. Moreover, distinctions should be made between developing a tool to be used in demonstration of satisfying generally accepted auditing standards and developing a tool to be used that actually works prospectively.

In conclusion, modern AIS technology has the potential to allow internal and external auditors to use larger sample sizes (if not entire populations) that address and quantify with greater accuracy more types of errors and fraudulent conduct through, among other mechanisms, focusing attention on the usefulness and timeliness (i.e., relevance and reliability) of this powerful technology for the purpose of attesting to the accuracy and completeness of accounting data (Durney, Elder, and Glover 2014). These semi- and fully automated processes enhance both efficiency and effectiveness in monitoring conduct risk of individuals who may otherwise subvert the representational faithfulness of the reporting function, internally and externally.

Professionals, academics, and other stakeholders in the continuous assessment of the effectiveness, economy, and efficiencies of this expensive and disruptive commitment to AISs as a means of enhancing and empowering organizational recordkeeping, reporting, and performance measurement need to be mindful of the following persistent human resource requirements:

- Professionals embodying competency in public and managerial accounting skills are helpful to detect errors and provide assurance that the given AIS is up to date and to reflect any relevant changes to GAAP. Just as one size rarely if ever fits all, initial plans and programs need continual review for relevancy under current and expected conditions.
- Professionals embodying proficiency in public and internal auditing skills are helpful to detect error on a timely basis and to provide material assistance in the design, implementation, and remediation of fraud risk assessments applicable to the given organization in its particular industry or sector. Impartial examination of auditing feedback furthers constructive amelioration of the control system.
- Professionals embodying expertise in specialized or nonroutine auditing skills, including forensic and performance auditing, are helpful to test with challenging foresight and respond with rapid deployment circumstances that may otherwise be hidden and deleterious. While waste and abuse of organizational resources may be overt, fraud and corruption are frequently concealed and perpetrated with collusion between or among employees and agents.

- These professionals require the organizational commitment reflected in practice, including sufficiency of budget and supporting human and infrastructure resources, to perform their roles consistent with law, regulation, ethics, and other socially expected standards and demands. Mere lip service to accurate, complete, and timely prepared reports will not properly serve markets, regulators, or the civil society at large, notwithstanding the investment in technology such as computer-based AISs.
- As the AIS facilitates transnational organizations and activities that cross borders and jurisdictions, there is an unmet need for an effective global governance board that would fairly evaluate and control, if necessary, transnational transactions, giving due consideration to a nation-state's sovereignty. AISs impact the privacy and confidentiality of sensitive personal data and the protection of intellectual or other property rights. These rights and obligations should be harmonized and fairly developed and applied, if not uniformly so, and not dependent on the affected individual's venue.

Indeed, the control environments of transnational and other large entities would suffer without an AIS of sufficient capacity implemented and maintained by continuously monitored information technology, accounting, auditing, and fraud and forensic specialists. The AIS provides the power. However, the responsible individuals must possess the political and organizational will to act and make decisions with accounting and corroborating data under the imperatives of the integrity and ethics demanded throughout civil society. The AIS serves not only the embedding organization but the public at large that require the organization's products and services fairly prepared, delivered, and represented.

Thus, the AIS is a mechanism not only to solve principal-agent problems (e.g., failure of an employee to conform to managerial directives) but also problems demanding collective action solutions (e.g., failure to abide by financial regulation regimes). An organization owns not only the AIS but perhaps also what it facilitates and effectuates. In sum, the following effects of entanglement of the power of AIS and related technology are noted:

- First-order effects are those that impact the individual. The AIS changes what is demanded from individuals; their knowledge and skills should include facility with technology and accounting and auditing.
- Second-order effects are those that impact the organization. AISs expand what can be done, extending the breadth of enterprise and the depth of analyses of so-called big data through robust programming power.
- Third-order effects are those that impact society at large. AIS and related technology empower enhanced monitoring and measurement of performance, including the design and implementation of expansive surveillance tools, making it more likely that bad conduct may be detected timely or prevented entirely.

Those effects are not without detriments such as loss of privacy, lack of official forgetfulness that would allow individuals to recover from past misdeeds and not be held lifelong to indiscretions long past, and enhanced ability of concentrations of power and influence to maintain and expand upon their initial dominant position, resulting in an overabundance of conformism to the ideas and values of these concentrated levers of power independent of their effects on their subordinates. Again, who benefits and who loses by how much and for how long?

Five Key Applications of Accounting Information Systems

CHAPTER 1

Introduction to Accounting Information Systems

David M. Shapiro

Overview of Accounting Information Systems

As duly noted in the *New York Times* approximately 100 years ago (Wildman 1916), accounting methods are designed and implemented not only to prevent and detect fraud and error but to make realistic the successful administration of big business. Accounting information systems (AISs) were and are essential for preparing external purpose financial statements such as those filed for analysis in the public domain with the U.S. Securities and Exchange Commission (SEC) and for preparing internal-use proprietary reports to empower managerial decision making. These two types of objectives are not met identically: The information needed and developed for management encompasses that which is prepared and publicly audited for the benefit of external users such as vanilla equity investors in secondary markets like the NYSE but supplements it with granular and specially classified data that may allow management to enhance its own market position. This granular, special information is proprietary to the reporting entity. Thus, AIS serves both private and public ends.

AISs predate computers, and they have become more prominent and expensive as the decades have unfolded since the late nineteenth-century notoriety and dominance of trusts and big business in the United States

---

In memory of Abraham Briloff, whom I never met but whose understanding and reporting of analyses of financial reports and accounting statements are nonpareil.

and elsewhere. They have enabled real growth in private and public sector organizations, and they have facilitated materially misleading and fraudulent financial reporting and other criminal activities and civil wrongs. AIS is a tool, an instrumentality that is manipulated in satisfaction of human ambitions, for better and for worse.

The term represented by the acronym AIS comprises three words signifying three key concepts or variables introduced as follows:

- Meaning of system—an AIS is both a set of interrelated components of a physical process such as operational computer hardware and a logical process such as transformation of inputs into outputs under computer software applications. Systems may be closed and fixed by its rules of strict construction or open and flexible under rules allowing potential unlimited exception, illustrated by mere computing capacity to machine learning capacity. Systems are important for what they may include, such as records of cash receipts, and what they may exclude, such as updated financial status of borrowers.

- Meaning of information—an AIS processes raw data, whether digitized for input into computer-based systems or manually input into multicolumn hardcopy journals and ledgers, into higher order final form information for communication among designated parties. Information is important for what it may represent in fact, such as truthful transactions, or what it may represent falsely, such as fictitious transactions. Alternatively, information may not represent anything real notwithstanding the absence of bad intent. Information is code for communication, including potential obfuscation, propaganda, and so on.

- Meaning of accounting—an AIS provides manual, semiautomated, or automated processes operating under rules of accountability to prepare records and reports necessary for stakeholders, such as high managerial agents, regulators, and other users to understand reporting entity performance, using both financial and nonfinancial inputs. Accounting is a mathematically derived set of constructs establishing the history, prospects, and agency behind decision making and results of operations. It commonly relies upon double-entry bookkeeping (DEB), forcing compliance with predefined accounting classifications such as assets, liabilities, equity, revenue, gain, expense, and loss accounts. It may be factual or fictive, that is, with or without support by any real-world transactions.

Systems broadly include all information systems, which specifically include all AISs. However, some systems are not information systems, and some information systems are not AIS. Whereas we are fairly familiar with the general characteristics of weather systems, which are an example of a natural science system, and human resources information systems, which are an example of a design science system, the AIS is a special case of design science; that is, the information, rules, and processes are purposefully designed by system architects based on accountability principles generally, including special compatibility with requirements of generally accepted accounting principles (GAAPs). The AIS provides a key feedback loop to management.

AISs are characterized by strengths and weaknesses. However, they are always incomplete; that is, a given AIS relates to the potential rights and obligations of the reporting entity for which it exists. For example, transactions that concern the private sector corporation GE and its employees and agents will exclude transactions that concern the public sector organization City University of New York, assuming no intercompany transactions. More importantly, transactions that concern a given reporting entity may not be included within its AIS absent general or specific managerial instruction to do so. AISs are manipulable and self-serving. If the high managerial agents elect to exclude related party transactions, these transactions may likely, absent the highly creative efforts of the public auditor, not be recorded and reported as such. In brief, AISs may not be neutral tools of measurement but capacities dedicated in support of managerial goals and objectives.

Moreover, identifying an AIS's necessary attributes may not be clear. For example, a layperson presented with a hardcopy ledger of company accounts might conclude that it's ineluctably an AIS (albeit in manual form). However, what if the ledger does not conform to DEB; would it nonetheless comprise an AIS, or at least part of one? Additionally, how do digitally storing financial and transaction data change, if at all, the characteristics of the output information? Does the potential impermanence (or transience or malleability) of computer-based AIS data imply that there may be no unalterable and true history of the reporting entity; would the systemic and informational risks be intolerable under a computer-based system vulnerable to complete or partial erasure through intentional or inadvertent means? Resolution of these issues may be facilitated through an understanding of the history and evolution of the AIS.

History of Function and Use of AISs

Currently, efforts to deskill and reskill the labor workforce required to design, implement, and maintain AISs may be as disruptive as earlier efforts, implicating spreadsheet and database skill requirements for those working with AISs (Sy and Tinker 2010). An argument may be cogently put forth that the accountant, who is the primary but not the exclusive user of the AIS of his or her employer, is becoming more data entry clerk than required expert in DEB. Facility with the laptop computer and useful spreadsheet and similar applications (collectively, essential software) is the dominant skill requirement more so than transaction analysis demanding a deep understanding of DEB. In practice, the software may not require that the data entry clerk understand the transaction, unlike the traditional DEB accountant that needed to perform the deductive analysis of accounting against the records provided. The essential software has transformed the meaning of the essential employee or agent.

These recent developments did not arise from a vacuum. Research on AIS demonstrates that the discipline had been primarily viewed by academics as a blend of computer science, cognitive psychology, and organizational behavior (Poston and Grabski 2000), but AIS existed before the advent of computer-based processors. This is due to the informational needs of those directing the administration and management of commerce and government. Quality, quantity, and processing speed are materially affected by the evolution of computer-based technology, but the originating needs for such are longstanding.

Pre- to Mid-Twentieth Century (e.g., Manual AIS)

Using accounting to control the disposition of assets, including satisfaction of obligations to lenders and other providers of capital, routinely occurred well before computers became the primary required tool of persons in commerce. Importantly, with respect to accounting issues, computation of debts owed and profits retained remains not only an ancient problem but a current one, too. While DEB has been used for centuries, the question whether it is a necessary structure for AIS may be answered in part by examining how it functions in manual AISs that were the norm in commerce for centuries.

DEB requires both credit (right-side) and debit (left-side) entries for every transaction record, originally recorded in a chronological general journal known as the book of original entry and summarized by accounting classification such as cash, sales, and so on in a separate book known as the general ledger. Thus, the journal lists transactions by date, and the ledger lists them by type.

The accuracy, completeness, and timeliness of the reports potentially available and verifiable through public auditors or representatives of other stakeholders such as lenders under a manual AIS limit the quality of administration, including inspection and oversight, of the reporting entity. See Table 1.1 for an outline of some of the vulnerabilities and risks.

Table 1.1 High-level perspective of deficiencies of manual AIS

Accounting evidence	Initial balance	Updating	Audit capacity
Records	Manual entry errors in journal(s)	Accruals and deferrals overlooked	Limited ability to trace to reports due to incompleteness
Reports	Ledger incompleteness (from journal error)	Administrative inconvenience	Limited ability to vouch from reports due to costs
Analyses	High-level DEB understanding and skill	Limited drill down and root cause	Fraud and error risks due to inaccuracies and incompleteness

The deficiencies are clear, posing a risk to effective and fair administration. Stakeholders, including creditors, would be vulnerable to the limitations of the underlying accounting and corroborative data. Moreover, even the owner, especially where often absent from hands-on inspection and oversight of the business processes and accounting, therefore, would be hard-pressed to have significant confidence in a manual AIS, other than on a small and intimate scale. In brief, a manual AIS suffers from asymmetry of information risk; that is, the accuracy and precision of the outputs may not resemble economic and legal (true) reality as constructed by counterparties. Parenthetically, all computations, classifications, and indices of data prepared under a computer-based AIS could be theoretically performed by a manual AIS, given adequate resources such as accounting expertise, budget, and time to perform. Practicably, this is highly unlikely.

In further explanation of the asymmetry noted above, consider the following material elements of the AIS:

- **Records:** These comprise the building blocks of a manual AIS. Data contained within records corroborate journal entries and ledger balances. Auditors would vouch for the transaction processing of the auditee by reference to, among other sources of evidence, its records, and they would trace transactions from their records in books of original entry to financial reports such as general ledgers. This validates the integrity of AIS processing, comparing inputs to outputs and vice versa. A manual AIS is not merely labor intensive but may present a high risk of inaccuracy and incompleteness, contingent upon the expertise and resources available in the reporting entity, rendering the costs of preparation and compliance prohibitive.

- **Reports:** These comprise mid-level compilations and summaries based on the records. Recorded data are used to compile meaningful summary reports, including the general ledger, that articulate the reporting entity's financial position and results of operations, which are general purpose financial reports for external users such as government regulators and investors. Under a manual AIS, report generation is administratively cumbersome, requiring the accurate and complete accumulation and summarization of records of transactions, which would undoubtedly and practically be characterized by significant risk of error. Additionally, high-level accounting expertise, including facility with DEB, would be necessary to prepare meaningful, accurate, and complete financial reports on a timely basis.

- **Analyses:** These comprise the high-level dissections of data such that important issues may be examined with intelligence and information. Taking basic financial statements such as balance sheets and income statements and breaking down their components into particular objects of focus such as accurate and complete costing of goods and services would require significant financial sophistication and familiarity with the specific manual AIS in place at the reporting entity. Additionally, a significant volume of clerical resources would be invoked to obtain, organize, summarize, and format the data into transparent manual reports such as multi-column ledger paper for analysis by the accountant. A review for accuracy and completeness would necessitate significant expertise with DEB, assuming preparation under DEB. Also, experience at a given reporting entity may not be readily transferable to another reporting entity (a potential impediment significantly less likely where off-the-shelf AISs are used).

DEB was and is perceived to comprise a necessary part of checks and balances to prepare sound financial statements, whether for internal or external purposes. However, it is not intuitive, requiring at a minimum an apprenticeship with professionals proficient in its application. While many things may have changed a bit, DEB is still widely practiced and is an essential part of the education and training of the certified public accountant (CPA) (and bookkeeper). Also, it is virtually inconceivable to imagine an AIS not inextricably computer based. The logic, deduction, and mathematics of DEB are highly compatible with the strengths of computer-based dynamics and processing.

Late Twentieth Century (e.g., Computer-Based AIS)

Some academics have made the distinction between coarse and precise (accounting) information systems and their effects on managerial honesty

(Abdel-Rahim and Stevens 2018). Computer-based AIS facilitates the development and implementation of a potentially fairly precise information system compared to the rather coarse or primitive manual AIS of earlier decades. Managerial assumptions and estimates may be accurately and precisely calculated and extended over long terms. For AIS purposes, precision means the system allows for the preparation of a range of values closely correlated with their true (objective) values.

For management generally and users of AIS specifically, the recent decades have been characterized by a focus on business intelligence to minimize costs and obtain benefits of computer-based expertise independent of the alternative, which would be a dedication of numerous labor hours by CPAs and specialists in AIS work product accuracy and completeness. While these tools, which are primarily algorithms using fixed and flexible procedures, including artificial intelligence and machine learning, to solve problems arising from the integrity of accounting and corroborative data, may be more feasible for large enterprises rather than small entities due to their cost and implementation requirements, including training clerical staff in their effective use, they may fairly be described as both an improvement over manual AISs and an inchoate solution to the problems inherent in computer-based AIS. The potential benefits of evolutionary AIS are considerable.

Table 1.2 outlines some important contrasts and current issues arising from the movement toward expanded computer-based (automated) AIS.

Table 1.2 Manual and automated AIS effects on levels

Level	Manual AIS	Automated AIS	Reconciliation
Micro (employee)	Inadequate human resources; high risk of error	Inadequate analytical resources; superabundance of data	Lifelong learning including continuing professional education (CPE) and training
Meso (employer)	Costly segregation of duties	General and application control problems	Employee turnover and unpredictable market demand
Macro (civil society norms)	Policy based on anecdote and salience of evidence	Big data issues including lack of privacy	Restructuring profit taking and general welfare

Undoubtedly, there have been risks avoided with the advent of computer-based AISs, including the capacity to analyze much more information (also known as big data) in a fraction of the time needed in manual AISs. However, the trajectory should not be interpreted as an unlimited and exclusively increasing trend of progress. Consider the following:

- Micro-level effects are those on individuals such as employees and agents. These natural persons (i.e., not corporate and artificial) bear the brunt of learning and relearning their jobs and underlying processes as technology morphs from pencil-and-pad to laptop-and-keyboard. However, it has not stopped there. Training and retraining increase costs, risk of error, and inefficiency in performance.
- Meso-level effects are those on employers, including corporations privately held or publicly traded. The tools available to management are imposing: Detective controls such as electronic surveillance and monitoring of employees through computers, peripherals, and so on offer potentially wide coverage; preventive controls such as access and permission levels with respect to the AIS equipment reduce the risk of fraud and enhance the integrity of accounting information. Direction and control over labor are routinized and expanded.
- Macro-level effects are those on society at large, including public and nonprofit sector regulators and supervisors. Initially, the prospect of big data and informed and effective public policy seems unavoidable in a rational choice world. However, we are not there yet. Cultural politics in the United States and elsewhere do not seem to require consistently any specific data for a given policy; rather, policies are too often agenda and influence driven, data or data be damned.

Twenty-First Century (e.g., Beyond Double-Entry Bookkeeping)

There is no shortage of research regarding the development of information technology (IT) tools to detect fraudulent financial reporting (Abbasi et al. 2012). Computer-based techniques have successfully invaded most aspects of management, especially and directly AIS, providing complex applications to record, report, and analyze data. AIS can accurately ma-nipulate populations of data, far exceeding the capacity of manually de-pendent AISs. However, first and foremost the AIS must have the capacity to integrate reams of historical data and differentiate among these data to prepare specialized reports on demand, hence the proliferation of data warehouses.

In contrast to natural science objectives, design science such as AIS has the objective of describing with sufficient detail the results of prior financial and economic transactions with counterparties, including share-holders of the reporting entity. Its focus is human agency and decision theory, and its goals are accuracy, precision, and completeness. It relies on the proper coding of rights and obligations in the relevant jurisdic-tions in which the transactions are governed externally and in which the accounting standards-setter pronouncements such as those emanating from the Securities and Exchange Commission and Financial Account-ing Standards Board in the United States are properly reflected. Thus, the proper design and implementation of AIS implicate not only consist-ency with internal evidence such as entity-stored records but validation through external evidence supportive of the objective state of rights and obligations in relation to counterparties to contracts, including customers and vendors.

While the future is to a significant extent unavoidably surprising when it finally unfolds in the continuously approaching present, the role of the accountant in the maintenance of AIS may change, sometimes abruptly. Whether this entails a flight from DEB, which would comprise a radical departure from centuries-old practice, or mere deskilling and reskilling of the accounting and IT workforces, which seems more likely, especially in the short term, cannot be entirely foreseen at this point. However, the potential costs and benefits of so-called big data will coerce change. The following trends and contrasts should be considered as at least relevant, if not probative of things to come:

- **Single-entry bookkeeping versus DEB:** So long as accountants are the primary users of AISs, DEB may persist for years to come. However, the influence of evolving software suggests that DEB is not strictly necessary to maintain records, prepare reports, or conduct analyses. The accounting logic underlying DEB is a hard habit to break from the perspective of accountants, including their trainees. Breaking loose from the DEB hold may entail redefinition of basic internal controls such as segregation of duties, which could be further subdivided at the (original) journal entry level. The contingency of DEB, while longstanding, may not be permanent.

- **Big data and unstructured data:** Transforming voluminous unstructured data like e-mails, analog recordings, and so on into a manageable pool of big data is a highly desirable objective that is not necessarily and practicably out of reach. The efficient integration of such corroborative data would elevate accounting analyses to a higher plane. This would also facilitate comparatively inexpensive forensic inquiries and investigations, reducing the need to hire outside specialists for evidence gathering and analysis. While deskilling the forensic process, it extends and routinizes these truth-discovery and accounting control practices.

- **Cloud computing and shared services:** There's a trade-off between economic convenience of outsourcing data storage and processing functions versus privacy and security interests of the reporting entity. To the extent that small and medium-sized enterprises can obtain the benefits of AIS services and functions that would be cost prohibitive if purchased individually, the trade-off would seem to balance in favor of the expansion of cloud computing and shared services, especially in environments where law and policy furthering data protections are weak. However, costs, including those following the realization of security and confidentiality risks, should not be understated.

- **Automation of the auditing functions:** This could significantly enhance the quality of AIS reports, especially where real-time auditing becomes routine such that the audit functions more like a preventive than a detective control. Clearly, quarterly or even monthly internal audits of transactions seem unnecessarily untimely in light of the potential of modern hardware and software: Real-time analysis may provide continuous rather than continual support of the inspection and oversight function. Moreover, mitigation of the garbage-in, garbage-out (GIGO) risk could prove cost-effective and helpful in mitigating in advance potential regulatory inquiries before these become injurious to the entity's reputation (Briloff 2001). Thus, internal consistency (i.e., validity of the information) and external confirmation (i.e., soundness of the information) become part and parcel of one integrated process of information flows.

Much has been done with IT and AIS. However, it is by no means complete, and we should perhaps expect the unexpected as we never step twice in the same river!

Distinguishing a Sound AIS from an Unsound AIS

Development and redevelopment of computer-based AISs have led to the creation of a new class of experts, namely, IT or systems technicians. These professionals have not entirely displaced professional accountants; instead, they have supplemented the pool of employees and agents to whom reporting entities must consult to solve business problems. Thus, having an AIS function in its intended way not only is key to getting business initiated, authorized, recorded, processed, reported, and analyzed properly but also enhances the processes and information flows under normal operations occurring without business interruption, which could prove costly and time consuming in light of the complexity of high-technology AIS and the shortage of tech-savvy skills among high managerial agents responsible for inspecting and overseeing business processes. Never has avoiding a technological problem (rather than merely awaiting it and then fixing it) become so essential. The skills are specialized and not inexpensive to procure.

The following observations are relevant to the discovery of the effectiveness of an AIS: Actual cases of feckless AISs may shed more light on the risks and pitfalls of AIS unsoundness than a set of abstract and unattached guiding principles. See Table 1.3, which illustrates some noteworthy and notorious accounting frauds implicating the reporting entity's AIS.

Table 1.3 demonstrates by way of significant examples that computer-based AISs have neither entirely prevented nor timely detected the risk

Table 1.3 AIS-assisted accounting fraud examples (estimated losses >$250 million each)

Entity	Issue	Detection	Resolution
Satyam (cybersecurity vendor) c. 2003–2008, based in India	Fictitious revenues, cash, and employees	Whistleblower pressure on chairman-CEO mastermind; CEO confession	Criminal convictions and public auditor sanctions
Toshiba (industrial conglomerate) c. 2008–2015, based in Japan	Early recognition of revenues: late recognition of losses	Internal auditors after long cover-up by senior management	Pending civil litigation by investors
Tesco (retailer) c. 2014, based in the UK	Premature profit taking; delayed reporting of expenses	Whistleblower pressure on senior management; internal investigation	Deferred prosecution agreement for firm with Serious Fraud Office; criminal charges against executives
ArthroCare (medical device supplier) c. 2005–2009, based in the United States	Channel (distributors) stuffing through fictitious sales of inventory	Internal investigation discovered prolonged executive malfeasance, including sham transactions and cover-up	Deferred prosecution agreement for firm; criminal convictions against executives
HSBC (financial institution) c. mid-1990s–2009, based in the UK	Willful failure to design and implement anti-money-laundering controls	Broad-based external criminal investigation by state, federal, and international regulators and law enforcement agencies	Deferred prosecution agreement; admissions of criminal breaches of executives' responsibilities
Société Générale (financial institution) c. 2005–2008, based in France	Fictitious trades recorded through overrides of supervisory controls	Internal investigation discovered prolonged executive malfeasance, including sham transactions and cover-up	Criminal conviction of trader; higher-level managers dismissed by financial institution

of accounting (control) fraud. The example of Société Générale may be especially noteworthy for the reported managerial toleration of overrides resulting in trading profits but not overrides resulting in trading losses (Baker, Cohanier, and Leo 2017). Profit does not launder a failure of ethics and due care in inspection and oversight.

However, the use of Excel in many small-to-medium entities as a key application supporting the disclosure and presentation of accounting information cannot be realistically perceived as a remedy. This is less a criticism of Excel spreadsheet capacity than a recognition and appreciation of the volume of transaction and data processing across domestic and international jurisdictions. Spreadsheets are not comprehensive AIS. Thus, the following types of problems remain:

- Does the AIS accurately and completely represent the actual internal business processes, flows of information, and decision making and record retention policies and procedures of the reporting entity? This is a question of validity of the AIS. Is there intrinsic evidence such that material exceptions and internal inconsistencies occur without timely detection and remediation? Is management even considering this risk?
- Does the AIS accurately and completely represent external business relationships and transactions of the reporting entity? This is a question of soundness of the AIS. Is there extrinsic evidence such that the records and reports of the reporting entity would reflect material conflicts and disagreements with trading partners, if known? How effective is management's due diligence?

Controlling conduct risk by employees and agents is one issue; most systems allow for high managerial agent discretion, which may be a desirable characteristic and superior to a system that does not admit such manual power to override. After all, management needs the power and discretion to remedy error promptly. However, more fundamental is the suitability of the AIS for a given reporting entity. Just as AISs are not identical in performance and capacity, reporting entities have distinct vulnerabilities and needs.

User Requirements

If the AIS works effectively and efficiently, the intended users should experience a demonstrable and worthwhile enhancement to their job performance. However, AIS may be expensive, with significant costs incurred up-front in the design, installation, and commissioning of the system, as well as the incurrence of the obligation to maintain the system. Buyers expect that these high initial and maintenance costs will be exceeded over the medium and long terms by the cost savings, especially reduced labor costs. In brief, more costly labor hours such as professional accountants' service efforts would be subsumed under a computer-based AIS contingent upon implementation with less-costly labor hours of clerks, with technical oversight by the principal accountant's office and IT and systems personnel. Additionally, the value added should be considered at both the organizational (entity-wide) and the political economy (regulatory) levels (McLaren, Appleyard, and Mitchell 2016). While organizational demands seem obvious as a consideration, regulatory demands may be given short shrift, an approach to be cautioned against in these times of globalization and far-reaching operation of law such as the UK Bribery and the U.S. Foreign Corrupt Practices Acts.

In brief, design expectations and actual performance may diverge.

- **Entity-wide:** The reporting entity needs accurate, complete, and timely data about its operations, especially the performance of employees and agents. Users from the rank and file and up in the traditional pyramidal structure of organizations provide inputs, monitor processing, and analyze outputs. They have different capacities and motivations. Thus, the AIS needs simplicity and intuitiveness like graphical user interfaces to the extent feasible. Generally, the level of user-friendliness bears an indirect relationship with the level of skill required of users such that a complex AIS may demand a higher skilled user, which may translate into higher labor costs and impair the expected net added value of the AIS. Therefore, a significant entity-wide issue is the adjustment of the AIS process to user skill requirements, with the desired result of overall lower costs and improved benefits over the medium to long terms. The risk is that deskilling and reskilling of users may impair expected productivity and effectiveness. A sound AIS allows ready use and interpretation with a minimum of reskilling demands and deskilling errors; that is, transitions and decision making are facilitated.

- **Regulatory:** The external supervision and regulation of reporting entities, if required in the given political economy, also needs accurate, complete, and timely data about reporting entities under their inspection and oversight responsibilities. However, trade secrets and other proprietary data may be excluded from disclosure by reporting entities under certain circumstances. This is a problematic gap. Untestable theories of trade secrets and related protective claims shield data from external validation. Regulators may fail, and society may be harmed under this structure of information asymmetry. Thus, AIS inputs, process, and output ordinarily remain separate and apart from regulators, which must depend on manually overseen and directed submissions from the reporting entities. This preserves the liberty of the reporting entity's management, but allows the perpetuation of bad conduct ranging from accounting control fraud to covert release of hazardous substances into the environment. However, the AIS needs configuration such that it may efficiently and effectively prepare reports and identify corroborating records consistent with requirements of regulators, including output in ready conformance with statutory accounting demands under regulation of the insurance and other industries. A sound AIS comports with regulator demands with a minimum of friction and burden induced by requiring the manual reprocessing of data.

The demands of users, including designs and implementations that enhance reporting entity profitability and support compliance with applicable regulation, exist alongside technological feasibility. Not all AISs are up to the task.

Capacity of System

There are two overarching potential obstacles: How does the preexisting or legacy AIS relate to the new and improved AIS, and how would anticipated growth and innovation such as contemplated mergers and acquisitions (M&As) relate to the AIS in place? Entities change, and demands on the AIS will vary.

- **Legacy constraints:** Often, an AIS is implemented into a preexisting AIS. These constraints are traceable to user requirements (see above) and system compatibility. Workarounds and other programmatic solutions to the limitations of systems in place may unpredictably and detrimentally impact the effectiveness and efficiency of the newly implemented AIS. Data quality and processing, including reliability and completeness of reports, may require significant real-time and end-of-period adjustments, threatening the viability and value of the new AIS. Having the ability to use deskilled and less-expensive labor hours to input and process data may not seem to offer the bargained-for benefits where more skilled and expensive labor hours are required to assure data accuracy, completeness, and timeliness. Potential data rehabilitation costs need consideration.

- **Growth and innovation:** M&A presents both new accounting and other information system demands such as the need for revised enterprise resource planning and revised enterprise risk management that may not be resolved in run-time (real-time) processes. Instead, these piecemeal outputs get ironed over in periodic roll-ups that require manual and technical inspection and oversight of information flows from disparate sources and systems, creating the risk that M&A problem solving related to AIS is more short term than medium or long term in focus, outcome, and effectiveness, in addition to the persistent lack of timeliness. The lack of compatibility among information systems, especially AISs, increases the friction in M&A, tending to impair the integration of employees and agents from different cultures with varying expectations. Unless the acquirer is willing to commit significant technical and economic resources in increased AIS repair and maintenance problem solving, the business combination would likely present an avoidably higher risk of failure. Compound these costs with the human tendency to cling too long to strategies characterized by a superabundance of sunk and unrecoverable costs, and fiscal and reputational disaster may shortly ensue.

While user requirement and system capacity technical and human resource issues are neither new nor obsolete concerns, the difficulty is in deciding the current state of the entity in relation to the AIS: How near or far is effective integration? However, progress may be made in the near term.

State of the Art

Few subject matters are as difficult to keep up with as evolving AISs. However, having the capacity to understand the origins and vectors of the fundamentals of AIS may be contingent upon recognizing the apt paradigm(s). See Kim, Gangolly, and Elsas (2017) for an explanation of, among other topics, traditional systems flowcharts and alternative Petri net models. To grasp the potential enhancements to automated AIS, an understanding of how to conceive or model it is necessary. Additionally, central to understanding the future path of AIS is recognizing the potential for the automation of the auditing functions. Briefly, accounting without auditing is too subjective and untested; the risks of error and fraud would be virtually intolerable. However, too much auditing layers unnecessary costs and other burdens on operations.

In brief, a Petri net models the flow of information between two nodes, namely, a place that stores information and a transition that makes decisions regarding these information flows. Thus, a place would include, for example, a master vendor database, and a transition (process) would include a state wherein, for example, a purchase order is approved or not approved. Places and transitions are distinct sets. Moreover, objects of data, such as purchase orders, are represented by tokens in Petri nets that flow from node to node.

Of course, there may be significant differences between the AIS as modeled and the AIS in practice, as well as the issue of validation of the information prepared as the output of the AIS. The long-standing worry of GIGO, while much less of a problem presently, has not been eradicated. Importantly, the task of modeling structure is different from the task of designing for practical effectiveness in all required dimensions. See Table 1.4 for an outline by which to approach broad problem solving in AIS redevelopment.

AIS comprises a significant capital commitment over both the short and medium terms under the expectation that across the investment horizon, long term included, the payoff in efficiency, economy, and

Table 1.4 An outline for AIS problem solving and AIS redevelopment

Measure	Human resources	Technical issues	Reconciliation
Efficiency of inputs (quantity variance)	Deskilling refocuses on capital	Assembly-line model demands broad surveillance	Producing more with less has real limits
Economy of inputs (price variance)	Low-cost workforce variable across the world	High demand for simplicity risks incompleteness and inaccuracy	Race to the bottom creates macro-difficulties
Effectiveness of outputs (favorability of outcomes)	Continual retraining for goal convergence	Proprietary nature of AIS precludes comprehensive validation	Stakeholder satisfaction requires inclusive focus

effectiveness would be realized, justifying the original assumptions and estimates. However, please observe the following caveats about these uncertain measures:

- **Efficiency of inputs:** The objective of squeezing more output from a given level of inputs may present operational issues. Reduction in the quantity of inputs such as labor hours to prepare the same or higher level of quality report depends on a well-planned information system, anticipating and having adequate programmatic flexibility to incorporate new types and sources of data. The initial quality and comprehensiveness of the data accumulation capacity and range of processing routines are summarizable as the rules of the AIS. These rules need to allow additional inputs such as internationally sourced data consistent with applicable data privacy law, as well as potentially new types of data such as those derivable from the Internet of Things (IoT) also consistent with privacy laws, to be characterized as sufficiently flexible. Otherwise, transitioning from one level of AIS to another may be impaired and may threaten required efficiencies. Additionally, confidentiality and security of information may be at risk, especially with IoT.
- **Economy of inputs:** The objective of lowering input costs given the expected level of outputs may ordinarily be met through the AIS. Substituting comparatively expensive labor with lower cost

labor depends on sufficient technological leverage from the AIS. This explains part of the appeal of an AIS. So long as the required information does not vary significantly over time, the AIS can function well enough, but troubleshooting usually demands highly skilled technical and accounting labor, which may not be in the business plan contemplating the benefits of low-cost input labor. Assuredly, most routine AIS functions such as journal and ledger maintenance are improved and allow deskilled labor to operate, if not also oversee, them, but the issue becomes nonroutine: How often must the AIS be repaired and maintained by more costly and higher skilled technical consultants and accounting specialists? To what extent are bugs in the system really behaving more like un-intended features of the system?

- **Effectiveness of outputs:** The objective of an AIS is not merely having output that follows the logic of the algorithmic process; the output must contribute to favorable outcomes. It must be relevant and current to the entity's objectives. Thus, having an AIS that readily produces fraudulent financial reporting, while satisfactory to fraudsters and careless auditors in the superficial sense, does little to further the legitimate business objectives. The AIS clearly allows for business expansion, including internationally. However, the issue of profitability is distinct and not without its critics such as those lamenting the enrichment of high managerial agents and owners of capital well above the value returned to the labor dedicated to the businesses. This managerial leverage from a distance may be unfairly exploited. Also, AIS output is materially different from organizational effectiveness such that organizational activities should be assessable against civil society norms by the AIS (e.g., see below on sustainability). These programmatic and data demands are complex and evolving.

Reconciliation of efficiency, economy, and effectiveness problems with potential solutions demands not only a flexible AIS but a generous and yielding spirit of management. Substitution of machine for an individual may be opportunistic and profitable for the reporting entity in the short term, but civil society requires a broader perspective. The state of the art of AISs is virtually solipsistic in some respects (i.e., the virtual reality contained therein may be detailed but bogus); however, integration with suppliers and customers is a progressive movement outside the proprietary shell of an entity's AIS. To date, the reconciliation of private capital and public interest is not complete in any material respects, though redesign of the AIS toward wider views of usefulness to civil society is at hand. For example, factors to consider impacting redevelopment of AISs include the following key concerns:

- **Artificial intelligence (AI) and automated auditing limitations and prospects:** High tech sensors could be applied in many contexts to enhance the ability of the auditor to obtain meaningful and ready access to more sources of data. This enhancement to inputting is also facilitated by vendors and customers providing necessary information about past and planned transactions. Moreover, natural language processing and machine learning assist in extracting required data from documents. Undoubtedly, processing capacity has increased immensely due to developments of more sophisticated and useful computer-based technologies. However, the validity and soundness of the outputs remain at issue: Routine inspection and oversight of the AIS by technical experts, including experienced auditors, seems still necessary to assure the control of the quality of information, especially where transparency may be questioned in cases of so-called black box algorithms. To the extent the AIS is adequately compatible with AISs of vendors and customers, the audit functions of confirmation and documentation are facilitated. Audit hours may be decreased and the required auditor skill may be simplified.
- **Sustainability and qualitative data:** The AIS as a more inclusive repository of information is technologically feasible. However, its inputs, were they to include entity and industry impacts on the environment and society that are initially qualitative, such as a widely shared perception within the community that a noxious odor seems to pervade the local environs, would become relevant not only to the entity but to the embedded community at large. Corporate sustainability accounting seems more necessary than desired by decision makers within reporting entities like many other administrative costs without the readily demonstrable favorable

effect on profits. However, in their capacity as investors in capital improvements and in more robust and inclusive AISs, the social desirability of such enhanced information systems may trump individual desirability. Liberty is occasionally justifiably limited for public nuisance concerns such as those manifesting themselves as polluting by-products of the entity's operations. The practice of externalizing effects such as pollution is not sustainable over the medium or long terms notwithstanding the lack of a short-term charge against earnings due to failures of regulation and measurement. Failure of regulation does not ethically justify failure to maintain high standards necessary for the community at large. The AIS as traditionally construed is a repository for proprietary data of the reporting entity, but effects from business activities of the reporting entity are often not proprietary but public, such as water pollution. A higher level of accountability may be designed and implemented under an enlightened AIS in cooperation with civil society and the public sector. The AIS may ameliorate social ills and further entity profitability.

AI generally as a method and tool and sustainability specifically as an entity-wide and civil society–wide goal may form the blueprint for an integrated network of AISs that furthers individual, employer, and community at large objectives. Rollout of an AIS that incorporates sustainability accounting requires both organizational buy-in from the top-down and the appropriate content, such as sharing correlations between monetary and physical measures (for instance, costs of carbon inputs and expected costs of mitigating adverse impacts of carbon emissions) (Zvezdov 2012). A critical mass of acceptance and implementation may be necessary as in all effective networks such as the Internet; however, this issue of political will is distinct from the technological possibility and desirability, both of which seem essential in support of civil society.

Review and Wrap-Up

This chapter has provided an introduction to and overview of the meaning and application of AISs in the United States and internationally.

Technology's only boundary is affordability. Moreover, computer-based AISs have not eradicated the risks of misinformation (unintentional error) and disinformation (intentional misrepresentation). Nonetheless, AIS has leveraged clerical capacity such that it may be applied toward problem solving in accounting and other contexts requiring the analysis of financial (and nonfinancial) information. However, some caveats should be considered (see Table 1.5).

Table 1.5 An outline of caveats regarding AIS capacity and application

Factor	Hardware	Software	Labor
Costs	Large initial investment (purchase or lease)	Routine maintenance and debugging	Reskilling and deskilling of workforce
Benefits	Long-lived and predictable tangible asset	Continual capacity enhancement of programs	Less-costly labor hours displace more costly hours
Risks	Commitment to deficient infrastructure (e.g., obsolescence)	Defective algorithms (e.g., ineffective, insecure)	High turnover of necessary labor; lack of workforce commitment

Costs

While the expected benefits of AIS are rarely unstated or even understated, there are unavoidable, marginal costs that should be addressed before committing to a change in the AIS in place. These include the following:

- **Technology resources:** Training is required, and long-term strategic planning is necessary. Don't reflexively and thoughtlessly believe the hype: Expensive capital improvements may be beneficial, but they won't turn around a losing venture. An AIS does not usually turn loss into profit without fraudulent intent.
- **Human resources:** More training is required. Not only must users be expected to learn how to implement the AIS properly, they must also recognize well-publicized risks such as the threats of hacking and social engineering. Cybercrime and other wrongdoing accomplished with or through the computer is on the rise as the utility of computer-based AISs becomes more available and accessible remotely.

However, there are resources, including professionals with relevant credentials, available to assist in the mitigation of the risks emanating from the sources identified above. These include:

- **AICPA-Certified Information Technology Professional (CITP):** The AICPA is a recognized leader in the provision of public accounting and related services, including IT management and assurance (AICPA 2019).
- **Chartered Global Management Accountants (CGMAs):** The CGMA designation is well respected globally and maintains a business partnership with the AICPA.
- **(ISC)^2:** This reputable organization offers credentials and continuing professional education in many disciplines under information systems, including leadership and operations, IT administration, cloud security, risk management frameworks, and software security.
- **International Association of Privacy Professionals (IAPP):** This respectable nonprofit organization provides credential and continuing professional education in disciplines related to privacy and data protection. Globally, it has business relationships with similar organizations supporting the same mission.
- **Information Systems Audit and Control Association (currently known as the ISACA):** This organization offers, among other information system certification programs, the Certified Information System Auditor credential. The ISACA has a global and long-standing presence in the IT field, including promulgation of the Control Objectives for Information and Related Technologies (COBIT) framework for information systems' internal controls.

Though these costs are manageable for many entities, especially large enterprises, they may impede the advancement of small- to medium-sized enterprises, imposing a financial barrier to entry and redevelopment beyond their means. To a significant extent, this is highly unfortunate as creativity and novelty are often produced in smaller enterprises lacking overcontrolling bureaucracies so common in larger enterprises. Nonetheless, anticipated costs should not be examined independently of expected benefits.

Benefits

Modern commerce and public sector organizations cannot function well and accomplish their missions without an accurate and complete AIS that provides relevant and actionable information on a timely basis. Large organizations are facilitated by efficient AISs. The output or information provided may be reviewed under the following broad criteria:

- **Quantity of information:** Computer-based AISs may receive previously unimaginable volumes of data, which may be processed efficiently where hardware capacity, software relevance, and sources of affordable electricity are sufficient to the tasks demanded. In practice, increasing the capacity leads to increases in information processing. A well-designed AIS allows for more seamless integration of disparate entities (or nodes) within the global enterprise. The enterprise's AIS is the primary tool by which the enterprise is defined internally, described externally, and assessed independently. It permits an empirically supported, broad-based, and socially acceptable interpretation of the enterprise, assuming sufficient attention is paid to data formatting across platforms.
- **Quality of information:** Computer-based AISs, while not immune from the hazards of the GIGO principle, facilitate decision making from the top-down and bottom-up; that is, the range of information available to decision making throughout the enterprise may be enhanced by the AIS, allowing directors, officers, managers, and supervisors to obtain a superior sense of both the state of the constituent entities and the integrated enterprise. The quantity of information leads to the enhancement of the quality of decision making, disclosing, and presenting comparable information across the enterprise and consistent information from historical periods. Staleness and irrelevance of data, which comprise severe impediments to the quality of information, are mediated by the AIS, expanding both the domain of historical data and the reach of current data.

As both the volume of information extends the reach of the enterprise and the currency of data enhances the quality of decision making within the enterprise, the AIS and its technicians and technocrats gain increased leverage particularly within the enterprise and generally across civil society through the methodology and results of their decisions (e.g., the calculated and strategic move to outsource labor). However, dependence on AIS data is not without its detriments.

Residual Risks

AISs have been implemented in private and public sector organizations for decades. They have bred leadership by technological means under the inspection and oversight of technocrats, supported academically and in practice by the theory of the superiority of data-driven or empirical research. Though it seems that a well-functioning computer-based AIS using numerous measures of many variables offers more flexibility in reporting and more accuracy in recording of data in support of improved decision-making quality over the formerly widespread practice of figuring out the enterprise with multicolumn accounting worksheets (or even electronic worksheets prepared with less-robust databases than those available presently in advanced database management systems), these enhanced automated and semiautomated processes may be associated with unfortunate results, such as the following:

- **Effects on highly skilled workforce:** Computer-based AISs may privilege a certain group of technocrats over groups possessed of softer knowledge and skills not observable with measurements routinely used in these AISs such as managers relying on personal observations. The excess demand for and privileging of technical skills relevant to the use of computer-based technologies works an imbalance in the operation, inspection, and oversight of the enterprise as accumulating and interpreting data as a primary skill set tend to supersede the skill set requiring the cultivation of social relationships and professional networks.
- **Effects on less-skilled workforce:** Computer-based AISs may corral knowledge and skill development into presently useful niches relevant to hardware and software production but not broadly useful to address and manage change. While the short term may

resemble the past, the long term rarely does: Organizations should invest not only in powerful and expandable AISs that account for and report their activities in affordably timely, reasonably accurate, and fairly complete ways, but also dedicate appropriate research and development into the management and motivation of the lesser skilled whose livelihood, self-sacrifice, and participation in the generation of profit should be appreciated.

- **Effects on customers and suppliers:** Computer-based AISs may inure these essential market participants to relationships with the serving enterprise that are more robotic, inflexible, and impersonal than desirable for a mutually supportive market-based political economy. The success of computer-based and robustly automated database management systems, including AISs, should not serve as an inducement to neglect social, hands-on, so-called heavy-touch approaches to negotiations and relationships with customers and suppliers lest these essential participants in the profit generation of the organization become alienated and depart. Light touch may be profitable in the short term but serves as an ineffective business practice over the long or even medium term.

- **Effects on civil society:** Computer-based AISs may facilitate the sophistication and concealment of criminal activities such as global money laundering. Given the attention placed on money laundering schemes and asset recovery by the U.S. Department of Justice, there is little doubt that money laundering and its predicate offenses such as fraud and tax evasion, as well as violations of the Foreign Corrupt Practices Act, have become an indicator of the failure of the enterprise's AIS to both prevent significant unlawful activity and detect on a timely basis significant criminal activities. An AIS is not merely an engine for profit but a tool of compliance with organization- and society-specific goals and objectives, including law, regulation, and ethics.

As tempting as the belief that the future will resemble the past is, the predictability of the pathway(s) to be taken by society under the leadership of technocrats deploying AISs and other computer-based information systems in support of their individual and society's goals and objectives remains an elusive challenge. The enhanced technologies such as modern AISs offer not only increased power, leverage, and discretion, but also pathways for more timely and effective monitoring for accountability. However, planning for a profitable and desirable pathway is not automated but must reflect the commitment and action of virtuous moral character and circumspect political will. These are not necessary consequences; they are contingent on ethical and farsighted leadership.

Further Studies (Introductory Comments)

Noted below are important subtopics related to AISs, which will be addressed in more depth in future chapters. Their relevance to the broader subject matter of this chapter is noted; however, the meaningful depth required for these subtopics awaits further research, analysis, and reporting by this author.

Understanding Enterprise AIS

Enterprises are generally alike; that is, they buy, process, and sell items of value to customers, usually on trade credit, for financial resources. This cycle of commercial activities has been fairly constant over the years. However, entities are not identical; they have different strengths, weaknesses, and focuses. Thus, strategies by developers of AISs to create and sell an off-the-shelf similar product to all enterprises will not work industry or sector wide. Also, modular systems create their own disadvantages such as a piecemeal approach to client businesses and dependence for effectiveness on the tech savvy among the buyers' employees, which may vary from buyer-to-buyer.

E-Business and AIS

In brief, the Internet and supporting AIS within entities comprising endpoints of the supply and value chains empower both the consumers' and the sellers' bottom lines. E-businesses, including Amazon, have changed the landscape of commercial activities. However, these changes in technology and consumer habits need continual review and revision of coordination of entity AISs. Competition demands no less.

Internal Controls for AIS

Real-time processing validity and other data analytics are key domains for further enhancement through evolving AISs, including the use of AI. As AIS compliance becomes more dependent on the knowledge and skills of IT professionals and less dependent on accounting professionals, the tendency to become check-the-box inspection and oversight due to a lack of deep understanding of the meaning of accounting concepts, the entity becomes vulnerable to breaches of the spirit of controls and not necessarily the letter of controls. This form over substance encourages the wrong focus.

AIS and the U.S. Health Care Industry

The extent to which AISs affect the health care industry in the United States cannot be understated. Moreover, its positive effects on the financial performance of physicians (among others) have been reported by academics (Eldenburg et al. 2010). A key factor in experiencing improved outcomes and outputs is the degree to which key stakeholders, including physicians and other providers, are involved in the development, implementation, use, and maintenance of the AIS. Of course, the common dependency of care providers on third-party reimbursements, including Medicare, Medicaid, and private sector health insurers, creates a poignant need for a robust billing system with the AIS.

The subtopics noted above, while reflecting individualized efforts of research and explanation, should be interpreted as part and parcel of an integrated set of exploratory chapters on AIS that are best read in sequence and in their entirety. Until then...

CHAPTER 2

Understanding Enterprise Accounting Information Systems

David M. Shapiro

Introduction

Enterprises are organizations that need to account for their trading activities; that is, they obtain inputs for internal processing and then exchange and transfer these more or less transformed inputs for value, usually represented by financial resources such as rights to cash, to an independent entity at arm's length. These are exchange transactions. Both parties to the exchange are obligated to a certain extent, depending on the applicable jurisdiction, to account for the consumption and acquisition of resources and changes in status of resources resulting from these transactions. As the accounting is deductive (i.e., resources are exhausted or transferred to counterparties) and additive (i.e., resources are created or obtained from counterparties), the computation of changes is readily performable by computer-based technology; specifically, enterprise accounting information systems (eAISs). Enterprise records and reports are prepared, maintained, and updated within the logical structure of the eAIS, and employees and agents of the enterprise are made accountable through processes dependent on the eAIS. Thus, eAISs are designed to automate organizational processes and share data—both sourced in historical records and maintained in real time (Spathis and Ananiadis 2005). Generally, the overarching goal of using an eAIS is to enhance efficiency and effectiveness in decision making.

Neither the needs of user enterprises nor the products and services made available by eAIS purveyors are invariably in sync and aligned; that is, market requirements and product availability continually evolve. Moreover, successful integration of the eAIS demands significant adaptation of the technology by the employees and agents of the organization (Mu, Kirsch, and Butler 2015). While the technology is automated, the users are not.

Understanding the general concept and specific application of the eAIS requires different levels of skills contingent upon the individual's position in relation to the enterprise. It also requires a vision of the enterprise's activities comprising its value chain, as well as an abstract understanding of enterprise, process, and task levels within the enterprise that explain how the value chain is accessed and how its benefits are maximized in relation to competitors. That is, what resources, owned or outsourced, are available, what business events are necessary, including pre- and postsales, and who are the agents and employees using these resources within these chains of events, creating the cycle of value received to value added to value received and so on (Geerts, McCarthy, and Rockwell 1996).

As the goal of an eAIS is the improvement of the functioning of the enterprise through an efficient, economical, and effective integration of the various and interrelated business processes, an understanding of the eAIS generally demands knowledge of how it operates (i.e., the mediator variables) and what promotes or impairs the quality of its operations (i.e., the moderator variables). In brief, this chapter is presented as a summary discussion and analysis of key variables, common problems, including hazards and risks, and pathways for solutions, including strategies and tactics, regarding eAIS. While the technological tools of eAIS may seem to change abruptly and disruptively, their actual and potential effects on enterprises and the individuals who support these enterprises are not entirely unforeseen or unforeseeable.

Table 2.1 provides an overview of this chapter's approach, which is described more fully under each itemized section. Importantly, design, implementation, maintenance, and enhancements of eAIS should not be interpreted as an exclusively internal issue for the given enterprise. The conditions and effects arising from the application of eAISs in commerce

Table 2.1 Approaching eAIS in an uncertain environment

Factors	Macro	Meso	Micro
Resources	Laws and regulations favoring capital	Enterprise commitment to improvement	Realistic budgeting and scheduling
Events	Accounting standard-setter favoring industry	Value chain commitment to flexible relationships	Quality of real-time information and communication
Agents	Flexibility and creativity of workforce	Integration of employees and contract labor	Goal convergence among participants, major and minor

and government presently demand an integrated and holistic perspective and analysis.

Thus, the general accounting model recording, processing, and reporting inputs regarding resources such as capital assets, events such as transactions with customers, and agents such as employees is affected by conditions at the macro (e.g., societal), meso (e.g., enterprise), and micro (e.g., high managerial agent) levels. These conditions and effects percolate through the eAIS and should be properly valued. Both mediator and moderator variables are impacted by interactions at and across these levels.

Analysis of Mediator Variables

An eAIS depends on the presence and effectiveness of the following mediator variables to work as intended:

- **Adequacy of human resources:** The individuals who operate, oversee, and inspect the eAIS, including high managerial agents, other employees, and necessary agents such as independent consultants, require familiarity with the design system (i.e., the strengths and limitations of the eAIS). While compartmentalization is a common practice of enterprise operation, with many components operating without understanding other components, this division of labor and capital assets creates hazards and conflicts. For example, a budget may be prepared under significant influence of the finance division that fails to consider sufficiently the needs of the production and sales divisions. A plan to cut costs by near-sourcing (e.g., inputs and processes dependent on agents in Mexico for a U.S. enterprise) or outsourcing (e.g., inputs and processes dependent on agents in the Philippines for a U.S. enterprise) may detrimentally affect the quality controls and scheduling needs of the production division and result in failures to meet customer demand of the sales division.

- **Adequacy of financial resources:** An effective eAIS requires maintenance, including training and testing, that consumes financial resources beyond the initial capital outlays and recurring finance charges. While the system may cut some costs (e.g., employees needed in the treasury and accounting divisions), it creates others (e.g., specialized inspection, oversight, and training costs). Also, the types of problems that invariably but unpredictably surface such as application bugs not ironed out by the eAIS vendor are not readily solvable through customary managerial tactics: Forced overtime by the existing workforce may not substitute for the expertise of outside services not always immediately available.

- **Adequacy of capital assets:** The hardware and software comprising the eAIS require compatibility with one another and the retained legacy components as well as fitness for the purposes of implementing the eAIS; that is, meeting data input, process, and output requirements and solving optimally the routine and nonroutine problems of the enterprise, including consideration of the effects of the regulatory inspection and oversight regime. The evolving technology through which eAIS is accomplished requires that enterprises be prepared to commit to unpredictable updating requirements to remain current with the state of the art, as well as competitive with the enterprise's market.

Moderator Variables

The following moderator variables significantly influence and promote the quality of the operations of an eAIS:

- **Favorable climate at the macro or societal level:** For example, the jurisdiction's tax policies would affect the investments, commitments, and strategic plans of enterprises. Policies that promote risk-taking such as allowing generous or accelerated depreciation and amortization of hardware and software would encourage experimentation with enhanced but not widely accepted and proven technologies for enterprise development and redevelopment. Additionally, antitrust and related laws and regulations impacting the expansion of given enterprises would exert an indirect effect on decisions to invest or enhance expensive technologies. Unduly restrictive policies would impair economic growth and demand for highly robust eAIS technologies.

- **Opportunities for growth and enhanced efficiencies within and across industries at the meso or corporate level:** Although similarities and differences between industries and among enterprises cannot and should not be entirely eradicated, the extent to which functional equivalents are shared across industries and enterprises would indirectly affect the usefulness and effectiveness of commitments to robust eAIS technologies. Increased commonality would result in reduced opportunity costs (e.g., investment decisions are not either-or but enhance and enrich).

- **Innovative high managerial agents with a tolerant risk appetite at the micro or individual level:** Where stakes are high, individuals may be tempted to pursue the safer course of conduct, which may not be conducive to investment in high-value projects such as eAIS assessment, revaluation, and redevelopment. Moreover, individuals with preexisting high levels of success may be predisposed toward conservative strategies of preservation of wealth at the expense of high-growth business plans. To the extent that success breeds complacency and conservatism, those with lower levels of success but more drive to succeed at high levels may be the right individuals to lead eAIS projects.

Periodic review and revision is a necessary and time-honored practice among enterprises that achieve and maintain success over the long term. Enterprises that stand still are soon forgotten. Continual self-assessment is the rule determining the process and driving the information needs of successful enterprises; this would properly extend to the processes and tasks subsumed under their eAISs.

Assessment of the eAIS (e.g., Discovering Problems)

First, recognizing that an eAIS is not merely a system to report accounting data but is a system to initiate, authorize, record, process, and report, if necessary to external users such as regulators, corroborating data, which may include, whether by contingency or necessity, information flows not strictly relevant to the accounting data reported externally and internally, a fair understanding of a given eAIS should consider important social and legal issues, including privacy rights of employees, agents, customers, and other stakeholders. Moreover, beyond understanding how to maximize the operations of the eAIS is the issue of how the enterprise recognizes through external benchmarks or internally developed criteria of evaluation that its eAIS is state of the art and worth the investment.

While some researchers have used criteria such as the balanced score-card, which considers the four perspectives of financial, customer, internal process, and learning and growth, or fuzzy theory, which transforms qualitative data into quantitative data (Chang et al. 2011), to assess eAIS, this author argues that the criteria summarized in Table 2.2 should also

Table 2.2 **A general assessment approach to eAISs**

Criteria	Command	Control	Audit
Goals	Strategy is distributed	Centralized distribution of access	Inspection and oversight directed from board level
Objectives	Tactics are delegated	Centralized distribution of permission	Inspection and oversight managed at officer level
Tasks	Mission is actionable	Centralized distribution of review and approval	Impartiality assured through education and training

be considered, recognizing that overlap may exist between this approach and prior documented approaches in the literature. As the eAIS performs both risk analysis (e.g., the risk of money laundering) and workflow analysis (e.g., routine data reporting), it demands more than a simple rules-based approach, which may lead to too many false positives (i.e., type I errors indicating something might be deviant where it is not in fact deviant; Ai and Tang 2011).

Recognizing that garbage-in, garbage-out within the eAIS would invariably doom any enterprise, successful outcomes are contingent upon timely accumulating, processing, and analyzing the appropriate inputs. Thus, the criteria based on goals, objectives, and tasks beg the threshold question: Are the best, most meaningful data gathered routinely? Assessment of design science artifacts such as eAISs is different from assessments founded in natural science inquiries such as chemistry. The object of the natural (physical) science would exist independently of any human intervention, but the object of the design (managerial) science of eAISs is dependent on the assumptions and estimates forming the rules and processes governing the system and directing the flows of information across the system. This is not to suggest that eAISs are not subject to physical limitations imposed by prescriptive natural laws (e.g., the physics of electrical engineers), but the eAIS is an artificial work product: Its fitness for the particular purpose for which it was created depends on social context within the larger political economy.

At the risk of oversimplification, design science is data based and often affected by internally prepared (endogenous) inputs, and natural science is evidence based and developed from external (exogenous) inputs. Both of these types of sciences are often referred to as empirically grounded, and overlap may exist between endogenously produced information and exogenously produced confirmation evidence. However, their distinctions in sources and methods should be borne in mind as the soundness (i.e., truthfulness) and validity (i.e., logic) of their findings are examined and used (or not).

- **Goals:** Success, whether in the public or private sector, is a function of planning, executing, and good fortune. Generally, market dominance depends on understanding the strengths and limitations of the enterprise, its competitors, and the ambient political economy. Being an industry leader is knowledge-intensive, continually. Effectiveness of market penetration may be short-lived where goals are perverted (e.g., cannibalizing some customers for the benefits of other customers or short-term profit-seeking of insiders). Goals need to be supported with data that shed light on long-term dynamics of changes likely unavoidable in the political economy. For example, data sources such as the World Bank's GINI Index may be incorporated in the eAIS resource planning module to account for expected changes in the relevant political economies characterized by increasing or decreasing inequality of distribution of wealth (World Bank 2018). Such data are relevant for long-term pricing and production plans.

- **Objectives:** Success in accomplishing enterprise objectives, which are more short term and supportive of goals, depends on the integration of eAIS in the fabric of the enterprise; that is, the measurement system of the enterprise needs timely, accurate, and complete information as it records, reports, and checks its progress quarter-to-quarter, month-to-month, and more frequently as appropriate for the enterprise and its industry and supervisors and regulators. The strength of eAIS is its power to centralize key decision making—both strategic and operational—independent of the remoteness of the location of the units of the enterprise. The long arm, which reaches across geography and time, of eAIS enables prompt and useful feedback, so problems are identified and solutions are conceptualized well before they become unmanageable. The urgency of now no longer presents emergent conditions but presents opportunities for adjustments to tactics found not satisfactorily effective.

- **Tasks:** The fundamental level at which the eAIS demonstrates its value is in the day-to-day, routine processing of transactions and facilitating other necessary supporting activities such as treasury and finance functions for successful operation of the enterprise. While command and control, whether realized through automated processes such as access and permission levels or through centralization of the review and approval processes, provides high-level inspection and oversight of the enterprise's operations, there are too many employees and agents on whom the enterprise depends for effectiveness that cannot be adequately supervised through this high level. By defining and constricting decision making as much as feasible yet preserving the ability to create valid exceptions where necessary or expedient, the enterprise through its eAIS leverages its focus such that larger issues are discussed and analyzed at the appropriate high levels but routine issues are defined and managed such that employees and agent have no real option other than to converge their goals and objectives with the enterprise's goals and objectives. Task management is less discretionary with the individual.

Wrap-Up (Problem Solving)

There are many ways in which eAISs may fail, including inadequacies in data processing integrity, inadequacies in system security, or inadequacies in system structure (Li et al. 2012). Having the right system designed and in place may be somewhat unrealistic; having a reasonably cost-effective system for the routine and nonroutine issues foreseeably faced by the enterprise is a more manageable and less-expensive goal. As the eAIS is more than a labor-saving tool but is a computer-based technique for solving problems, often in real time, the foreseeability of the problem-solving potential of the eAIS should serve as an important heuristic (Table 2.3).

Table 2.3 Solving problems inherent to eAIS

Issue	Definition of problem	Framework of solution
Data processing integrity	Inputs are inaccurate, incomplete, and timely processed	Accounting control and operations high managerial agents review exception reports and line complaints
System security	General and application controls are porous	Information technology, security, and operations high managerial agents in committee review logical and physical design against comprehensive feedback
System structure	Architecture is not comprehensively integrated	High managerial agents in committee routinely review outputs and outcomes

Although eAIS has enabled bigness, management from a distance, and labor cost savings, perhaps the more important but less discussed issues are whether and how it has made managerial decision making more effective. The eAIS both prepares and computes using big data, a term used to describe the seemingly ever-expanding pool of information about everything that can be fit into computer-based storage. Algorithms are the principles through which the processing of big data occurs. To the extent they reflect predefined assumptions and estimates that may no longer apply (e.g., the so-called financial crisis and great recession beginning c. 2007 was exacerbated by the mispricing of risk and the application of unrealistic assumptions, including the failure to compute accurately the variable and dynamic trend of real estate prices and debtors' creditworthiness), the fact that the computer-based processing may proceed at lightning speed may serve more to hasten rushing to wrong conclusions and decisions than reaching well-founded and helpful guidance for meeting future conditions.

Thus, the old saw of measure twice and cut once should be taken to heart. Tomorrow's leaders need to be prepared to assess the algorithms and predefined processes constituting eAIS and not merely learn how to use and interpret off-the-shelf software applications. Whether to oversee routine business tasks such as journal and ledger preparation or to evaluate more complex risk assessments for money laundering and asset valuations, future officers and directors should not ignore the requirement to question and rehabilitate where necessary their eAIS and its superabundance of supporting applications and data on which it gorges and repackages such that the enterprise becomes transformed into a thoroughly informed and prepared, long-lived twenty-first-century success story.

CHAPTER 3

E-business and Accounting Information Systems

David M. Shapiro

Introduction

There is no fixed definition of e-business. It may be referred to as e-commerce. However, it is a term of art applied to enterprises and organizations, whether for-profit private sector businesses or governmental agencies, that rely on information technology (IT) and systems to provide goods or services, as well as to inform stakeholders about the results of operations and the financial condition of the enterprise or organization. E-business implicates IT professionals, accountants, and managers and staff at various levels in a mutual dependency network. The domains of knowledge and understanding required to conduct and support e-business are limited neither to the field of IT nor to the discipline of accounting or finance. As the system is integrated, so must the individuals needed to operate, inspect, and oversee it be holistically engaged.

E-business models range from enterprises using the World Wide Web primarily to inform stakeholders to enterprises using integrated web-based supply and value chairs among suppliers, customers, and the enterprise's back-office business processes and tasks (Kotb, Roberts, and Sian 2012).

Accounting information systems (AISs) are designed, implemented, maintained, remediated, and enhanced to further goals and objectives for e-businesses that may be identical, similar, or different from those arising from brick-and-mortar operations. However, many e-businesses operate and control physical infrastructure such as warehouses and administrative headquarters in support of their virtual operations. Thus, an e-business such as Amazon or Facebook does not discard generations of business leadership, skills, and knowledge derived from brick-and-mortar operations but builds upon these guiding principles and standards.

While this chapter discusses generally and broadly e-business and its AIS, the author does not intend to provide specific guidance to favor one platform and set of applications over another. *Caveat emptor.* Moreover, the inquiry should not focus so much on the best and right decision as obtaining sound value for the capital expenditure on the basis of the particular buyer's needs and environment. Sometimes, the luxury sedan gets stuck in traffic like the bargain compact car.

E-business may be best understood as a virtual brokerage using programs and data to mediate among users, advertisers, regulators, the intelligence community, or others in a computer-based network (i.e., the Internet) for the satisfaction of these interested parties' needs, desires, and missions. The e-business under its selected platform and applications supports ultimately the provision of goods, services, and data for the parties under its potentially global domain. In brief, it virtually brokers information between suppliers and users.

Note Table 3.1, which illustrates an approach to entering the domain of the generic e-business under the potentialities of an AIS, contrasting

Table 3.1 Approaching e-business through an AIS lens

Factor	Brick-and-mortar business and the AIS	E-business and the AIS
Accuracy of data	Perception may soften reliance on data	Fear and anxiety grow as data overwhelms
Completeness of data	The place of business as the focus for convergent thinking	The lack of place as a catalyst for divergent thinking
Timeliness of data	Time expands to fit work requirements	Time shrinks to fit stakeholder expectations
Security of data	Physical access controls over logical access controls	Logical access controls over physical access controls

key factors against a generic brick-and-mortar firm. The ideas are neither absolute nor invariable. Their application is contingent upon the specific circumstances of the given e-business or brick-and-mortar business, recognizing that a thorough vulnerability assessment would require a deep and empirical dive, which is not practical, desirable, or even necessary for this chapter.

While the profiling noted in Table 3.1 may be subject to indeterminate error, the analysis does not suffer from a lack of usefulness. Specifically, the following observations should be considered:

- **Accuracy of data:** E-business depends on speed of performance. Information systems, including the AIS, are its lifeblood. Data are reified as if concrete and not merely signals of the concrete. Inside the brick-and-mortar operation, employees and agents recognize the priority of the physical infrastructure, whereas the e-business is more an electromagnetic, virtually intangible web of relationships among nodes of suppliers and customers. In the e-business, data- and computer-based learning may be subject to fewer challenges than data and computer-based learning at the brick-and-mortar business. Sometimes, it is less what the data disclose than what the data don't provoke (e.g., deep analysis and unconventional and divergent reinterpretation of premises and reasoning) that greatly affects the quality of outcomes. Superabundance of data, especially a concern within the e-business, may take on a life of its own, dwarfing both the capacity and willingness of natural persons to question its meaning.

- **Completeness of data:** Neither e-businesses nor brick-and-mortar business may reliably make the claim that their data are complete. Moreover, attempts toward completeness may not be cost-effective and impair other goals such as timeliness of data. No business can stand still waiting for perfect information. However, the e-business is a child of the Internet wherein data may move at the speed of light and unencumbered by many of the physical constraints to which brick-and-mortar business are tied. Bandwidth greatly expands the portfolio of information available. Additionally, software applications, including electronic spreadsheets and databases, enable rapid processing, filtering, and extracting of material information. Whereas physical space constraints tend to confine, virtual space may loosen such constraints and liberate creative thinking and problem solving.

- **Timeliness of data:** Relevance demands timeliness. Business tied to brick-and-mortar infrastructure may adopt attributes of the fixed nature of its real estate: The natures of time and space merge into a more static framework than may be the case with the dynamic e-business that makes physical space secondary to the nature of virtual space. Broadband enables transmissions and processing of data and records at rates dwarfing any other medium. The constraint of timeliness shortens as more externally sourced and internally developed records can be processed with high-capacity information and communication technology, which is the modus operandi and first principle of e-business.

- **Security of data:** Lack of data protection and security may facilitate, among other crimes, identity theft (Tan et al. 2016). The data entrusted to the AIS inside the e-business control and custody are immense, personal, sensitive, and require due care by the e-business lest civil or criminal liability attach for failure to abide by sound data protection policies and procedures. At a minimum, physical and logical access and permission controls over the input, processing, and output domains are demanded. Without actual and perceived security in the information and communications technologies, confidence in the e-business on the parts of customers, suppliers, and employees and agents of the e-business would plummet and impair significantly short-term profitability of results and long-term sustainability of even moderately successful outcomes.

Thus, the AIS is necessary for competent functioning of e-business, and e-business imposes singular demands on the AIS. These factors characterize the complex and costly but ultimately necessary relationship between e-businesses and AISs: They are mutually supportive or destructive, depending on the capital equipment, public and private networks, and competencies of the employees and agents charged with design, implementation, maintenance, and inspection and oversight of these complex systems implicating other important stakeholders such as suppliers, customers, regulators, and the public at large.

With these concerns in mind, the question as to the potential changes in senior management, including the chief financial officer (CFO) role, influenced by the trend to e-business at the expense of traditional brick-and-mortar-based practices, remains a significant issue (O'Donnell et al. 2004).

Who controls the operations: Data or CFO? Undoubtedly, as business transitions from hard physical venues to soft data venues, management at all levels will need to refocus their skills and understanding to pilot the e-business with demanding AISs that will continually challenge management. New platforms require revisions in managerial approaches, including a commitment to continuous auditing in real time (Flowerday, Blundell, and Von Solms 2006).

While there is little doubt that AISs have improved the quality of information (e.g., see Liu et al. 2014), new problems may have arisen, such as information overload.

Risks and Mitigation

Among the more serious of potential problems afflicting the expansion of e-business are cybersecurity issues. Additionally, there are potentially groundbreaking changes to the professions of accountancy and public auditing, including less demand for bookkeeping and internal auditing skills. However, the potential for comprehensive review of transactions may support significant growth in the field of forensic accounting (International Federation of Accountants, International Accounting Education Standards Board 2018). Together, these changes comprise hazards with consequent risks. In outline, the risks arise at three levels: (1) the micro or individual level, (2) the meso or e-business level, and (3) the macro or civil society or regulatory level. An outline of a suggested approach to addressing these contingencies is presented in Table 3.2.

Table 3.2 A general risk assessment for e-businesses and AISs

Dimension	Micro	Meso	Macro
Data	Data are valuable like funds	Data are vulnerable like funds	Data are readily transferable without destruction
Programs	Algorithms may be readily misappropriated	Trade secrets are difficult to protect and monetize exclusively	Proprietary approach creates hazard of lack of interoperability
Research and development	Work for hire may impair creativity and research	Employees and agents cannot be completely controlled	Open source and public domain are inadequately supported

While no systems, manual or automated, are impregnable to committed wrongdoers, especially aided by conspiracy, collusion, or neglectful inspection and oversight, e-business and its AIS present particular vulnerabilities at various levels and across multiple dimensions. Recognition of the distinguishing features of the e-business, including its data, programs, and commitment to research and development, demands consideration of the interplay of these features with individuals (micro level), organizations (meso level), and the society at large, local and global (macro level). Before obtaining a fair understanding of risk, a knowledge of the structure of the material components of e-business operations and their keys to success is necessary, including the following:

- **Data:** These values comprise the units of analysis for both the e-business and its AIS. They are the traffic against which the e-business plays broker for its suppliers and customers. Data may be financial and readily subsumed within the AIS or nonfinancial and used, for example, as the added value of the e-business in tech companies like Facebook, for the benefit of advertisers and others, including customers. Data may be personally sensitive information and stolen for wrongful purposes by employees or agents; they may be taken by hackers through wrongful exploits; they may be diverted wrongfully to outsiders without deletion from the e-business's custody and care. In many respects data should be treated like financial funds information—valuable and not shareable without lawful justification and legitimate business purpose.
- **Programs:** These predominantly software applications comprise the tools through which manual processes and tasks are replaced with automated (artificial) intelligence techniques. The substitution of machine for natural persons in many respects mitigates risks inherent to dependence on individuals to perform required business activities. Error, including unfavorable outcomes resulting from such causes as fatigue, may be reduced. Outputs may accrue more efficiently and effectively. However, the program may be difficult to control. Theft of intellectual property poses a significant risk; wrongful communication of trade secrets may be effectuated through miniature peripherals and storage devices. Securing the program

while maximizing its usefulness may operate at cross-purposes, with effectiveness of employer-level controls over the program impairing both the user and the employee and agent experiences in its commercial efficiency.

- **Research and development:** While e-business and AIS are in many respects ideal complements (e.g., facilitating, filtering, sorting, and otherwise enhancing the communication of information at breakneck speeds), there are potentially serious medium- and long-term detriments. Specifically, the nature of problem solving through digital means is primarily binary, notwithstanding the potential benefits of machine learning and other realizations of artificial intelligence. The form of data processing through logical gates of either/or, and not, and so on does not map entirely the range of human intelligence. The future may not resemble the past. Also, for better and worse, employees and agents cannot and should not be utterly controlled, especially through digital means that are intrinsically impersonal. Moreover, a focus on proprietary profit taking may significantly neglect the public domain and public interest, resulting in the consolidation of income, wealth, and opportunity in too few hands. This would not bode well for innovation and progress within civil society.

E-business as the ultimate efficient virtual broker for goods and services offers the potential of tremendous improvement and convenience for the benefit of natural and artificial persons worldwide. The AIS embedded within the e-business is a key facilitator for making the transactions occur (e.g., order taking) and allowing timely, accurate, and fairly complete feedback as to the results of these transactions (e.g., real-time analytics). However, the risks inherent in these digital inputs, processes, and outputs lie in the displacement of natural persons such as employees, agents, and customers. This displacement may wreak economic havoc on the individual (e.g., job destruction) and drain businesses—both e- and brick-and-mortar—of the creativities embedded within the imagination of these lost individuals. Progress may not be readily programmed. More of the same may tend toward social decay and the resultant loss of business opportunity.

Wrap-Up (Problem Solving)

E-business, AISs, and further penetration of and dependence on information and communications technology require integration not only among the components of the hardware and software but also the employees and agents performing the key tasks, including inspection and oversight. The accountant cannot be content with knowing generally accepted accounting principles; the public auditor cannot be content with the skill of application of generally accepted auditing standards. The new platform of e-business demands a holistic and multidisciplinary approach (Hunton 2002). Silos won't work. Information feedback loops cover wide areas of the e-business (e.g., customers' demands, suppliers' capacities) and local performance metrics (e.g., profit and loss by segment and geography in real time).

E-business through leverage of its AIS demands creative thinking to address not only its hazards but its advantages. As e-businesses and their AISs facilitate increases in organizational size and complexity, they may inadvertently increase the risk of financial malfeasance and corporate wrongdoing, such as U.S. securities law violations. See Prechel and Zheng (2016) for a relevant application to the financial, insurance, and real estate (FIRE) sectors. The financial sector, which is highly dependent on digital tools like e-businesses, serves as a relevant, useful model for comparison. Digital processes may not dampen the risk of accounting-related frauds.

Moreover, neither e-businesses nor AISs should be interpreted in the common linear form of independent variable or dependent variable: In fact, e-businesses and AISs are both dependent and independent variables affecting each other and exogenous variables such as local economic well-being and the general welfare, as suggested by the competitiveness of municipalities and potential economic effects related to the efforts to lure Amazon headquarters into their venue (Casselman 2018).

As e-businesses are further integrated into the political economy, globally and locally, they may provide additional impetus to key accountability measures and movements such as the concept of triple bottom-line (TBL) accounting, the scope of which extends beyond financial reporting and managerial accounting for which the AIS provides material assistance in processing data and reporting performance metrics (Rodger and

George 2017). TBL, a measurement framework that includes economic, environmental, and social elements, may provide a wider and more useful lens through which to interpret and assess the for-profit, nonprofit, and governmental sectors' approach to and effect on profit and sustainability in the twenty-first century. E-business should not be excluded from the application of this framework, and AISs should be designed to accommodate this progressive and more robust approach to accountability of the effects of commercial and noncommercial operations and activities.

Importantly, design requirements for brick-and-mortar and e-businesses are mutually supportive, with both demanding full integration, including the incorporation of TBL. See Table 3.3.

Table 3.3 Integration of TBL into e-business

Function	Brick-and-mortar business	E-business	TBL integration
Fact finding (assumptions)	Personal interactions	Data recording	Robust mapping
Planning (estimates)	Unstructured conditions	Network effects	Full sensitivity analyses
Implementing (feedback and results)	Provision of goods and services	Coordination and feedback loops	Minimization of waste

Effectiveness and efficiency in performance of brick-and-mortar and e-businesses would be integrated with the social desirability metrics of TBL. The AIS, along with the internal accountant and public auditor roles, facilitates meaningful sharing of information. As e-business applications reduce the risk of human error and require higher-level inspection and oversight, commerce (and the operations and effects of nonprofits and public agencies) is measured and globalized to a hitherto unimaginable degree.

- Facts and assumptions are widely shared and deeply explored; the domain of the unknown and unknowable shrinks.
- Plans and forecasts are developed and revised with fuller participation among responsible parties and key stakeholders.
- Reports and implementation of performance metrics and feedback loops are readily available and in real time (or virtually close to it).

Caveats remain: E-business as a highly leveraged development from the exclusively brick-and-mortar entity will not be sustainable without diligent and competent human intelligence providing the inspection and oversight essential for civil society and its constituent for-profit, not-for-profit, and governmental institutions. The e-business, while providing for potent action, reaction, and feedback at a great distance (e.g., principal place of business in London with sales arms in New York City and Chicago and supplier feeds in Shanghai and Seoul), may tend toward perverted corporate narcissism unless anchored to facts and evidence on the ground. Importantly, data may not comprise reliable evidence where feckless or dishonest managerial oversight reigns.

Numerous threats remain: From undisclosed conflicts of interest to spurious corroborating data, the AIS may be used as a tool for concealment of bad acts. The AIS is not, to date, a self-executing program immune from machinations of integrity-deficient employees, agents, officers, and directors. It is an inseparable part and parcel of e-businesses; it should be redeveloped with such risks and threats in mind. Bringing buyers and sellers together in cyberspace through e-business applications is too valuable an activity for all stakeholders, public and private; standing still or doing nothing is not a feasible option. Evolution consistent with TBL metrics incorporated within the e-business AIS may be just the pathway required in today's global political economy.

A follow-up chapter relevant to these and similar issues will be forthcoming as internal controls for AISs are studied in more depth. After all, it is not merely power and leverage that e-business and brick-and-mortar businesses seek to maximize through their AISs: Effective actions should comply with the moral, ethical, and legal expectations wherever business operations are conducted throughout the globe. At all levels—from the individual to the employer to the community and society at large—business and its transactions should be held to sustainable, rational, and ethical standards of conduct.

CHAPTER 4

Internal Control for Accounting Information Systems

David M. Shapiro

Introduction and Overview

It is not merely power and leverage that businesses seek to maximize through their accounting information systems (AISs): Effective actions should comply with the moral, ethical, and legal expectations wherever business operations are conducted throughout the globe. At all levels—from the individual to the employer to the community and society at large—business and its transactions should be held to sustainable, rational, and ethical standards of conduct. At its core, the AIS serves as the key component in performance measurement (Djalil et al. 2017). The internal controls over and within the AIS comprise both its brakes and steering mechanisms. Moreover, material weaknesses in the AIS and its information technology present a higher risk of impaired financial reporting when measured against AISs and adequately functioning information technology (Li et al. 2012). In brief, the AIS is a key management tool, and internal control is management's set of techniques that function to direct the usefulness and reliability of the AIS.

First and foremost, the AIS is itself an automated control mechanism dependent on manual customization by management. Charts of accounts and other measurement tools are prepared. While the platform may be off-the-shelf, the AIS as implemented is importantly tailored to

management's ends. It is management's responsibility at all levels to design, implement, and perhaps most importantly revise the AIS to conform to the applicable standards for control, security, confidentiality and
privacy, and auditability. Specifically, the entity-level and activity-based
dependence of the AIS on control and audit via information technology elevates information system management to a high-risk managerial
concern (Sanderson 2013). In practice, the internal audit function of the
entity is primarily responsible for obtaining assurance as to the effectiveness of internal control over financial reporting and other processes.

Among the key standard-setters and reputable institutions for applied
research of internal controls as a function of internal audit include the
following organizations that directly impact the internal audit function
through influence over the profession and practice of internal audit or
indirectly impact the internal audit function influence over the internal
audit by independent (external) auditors.

- American Institute of Certified Public Accountants (AICPA 2019),
  which regularly publishes and updates best practice guidelines for
  members of the organization, including internal auditors, public
  auditors, and information technology professionals.
- Comptroller General of the United States (2011), which regularly
  publishes guidance on, among other things, audits, internal controls, and information system assessment. Its most recent revision
  of government auditing standards was published in 2011.
- Institute of Internal Auditors (IIA 2017), which published a set of
  attribute and performance standards in 2017, directly impacting
  risk assessment of internal audit and internal control.
- International Auditing and Assurance Standards Board (IAASB
  2016–2017), which published a set of principles in 2016 to 2017 that,
  among other objectives, guide the external audit function, including
  review and risk assessment of internal control of the client entity.
- Public Company Accounting and Oversight Board (PCAOB
  2017), which published a set of standards in 2017 that, among
  other objectives, guide the independent public auditor in evaluating internal control risk, including those arising from the AIS.

- U.S.'s Government Accountability Office (GAO), which published standards for internal control in the federal government in 2014, also known as the Green Book, describing internal control standards for the federal government.
- U.S.'s GAO, which published an audit manual for federal auditing of information system controls in 2009, which together with the Green Book would facilitate and enhance effective auditing and monitoring of AISs.

These macro-level, professionally recognized, and widely reputable standard-setters operate as not-for-profit organizations, guiding the profession of accountancy, public, and internal audit, whether the individual professional is practicing directly for clients in business or directly for public accountancy firms. They have long experience with issues related to internal control and AISs.

In overview, internal control comprises the set of features and properties that allow the AIS to be used by the entity as a reliable tool to achieve entity goals and objectives. Table 4.1 shows a summary overview of the

Table 4.1 Mediation of internal control through AIS

Domains	Inputs	Processes	Outputs
Records	Timely and accurate manual operations	Field checks for validity and accuracy	Clear and auditable cross-referencing between accounts and transactions
Reports	Routine and nonroutine transaction capacity	Integration of divisions for completeness	Timely real-time and routine feedback
Contingencies	Initiation and authorization functions	Predefined prompts for completeness	Default line items identifying entry or nonentry

framework of how internal control facilitates effectiveness of the AIS. It is not intended to provide a complete description of the relationship between internal control and AISs. However, it should stimulate thought for the purpose of design, implementation, and feedback from the AIS that helps to address issues of timeliness, accuracy, and completeness of the AIS. That is, is it made effective through application of the entity's internal control system?

Managerial responsibility for the design and implementation of internal control is not limited to the financial reporting function; it extends to all rules, processes, and information demands of the entity, whether arising exogenously from regulators and so on or arising endogenously from the conduct of employees and agents. The AIS is the set of automated tools and manual techniques that provide required information to the entity. It provides the foundation for decision making in the dynamic global political economy; thus, it cannot be realistically fixed in advance. It must allow for the addition of new modules and edit of preexisting modules. Models like maps need revision when the underlying terrain changes.

That reliable information is demanded and that it can be timely provided through effective AISs are not novel observations. However, the operating environment changes. From geopolitical risk to regulatory risk to conduct risk and so on, the need for internal check and control on the AIS—both to assure compliance with the intended original design and to obtain real-time data on adjustment to material changes in attendant circumstances—may be a continuously evolving problem.

Risks and Mitigation

The analysis of internal control as an independent variable producing an effective AIS begins with risk assessment by management (De Korvin, Shipley, and Omer 2004). Senior and executive management responsibility for this duty is ultimately nondelegable. Moreover, audit analytics provide substantial assistance to the internal audit and control function (Li et al. 2018). While macro-level organizations and standard-setters such as the Public Company Accounting Oversight Board (PCAOB) provide invaluable information and guidance for rules and processes, managerial responsibility is exercised at the meso level, leveraging the tools and techniques commonly accepted as best practices formulated and published at the macro level. Thus, the internal control structure and system may be interpreted as a means of directing the AIS to record, process, and report all of the essential data available from the entity's plans, operations, and analyses.

Internal control is management's objective; the AIS is a means of accomplishing this. There are factors that facilitate managerial control through the AIS; however, these factors do not operate without risk. Table 4.2 outlines these factors and risks.

Table 4.2 Factors facilitating and risks impeding internal control through the AIS

Factors	Security (tightness)	Flexibility (suppleness)	Errors and omissions
Directors and officers	Delegation hazard	Do-it-yourself hazard	Alienation from technology
Employees	Workaround hazard	Excessive sharing	Competition crush
Agents	Breach of contract	Openness vulnerability	Impersonal apathy
Others	Notoriety of success	Phishing and forgery	Ocean of opportunities

These risks arise from the structure of the entity and its AIS, including the use of continually evolving technology, and the limitations of different individuals struggling within distinctive civil societies across the global political economy. As natural persons are directed, controlled, and displaced by machine learning tools and other artificial intelligences, their capacity to thrive in commerce is strongly affected by the ability to adapt to roles requiring the development of new skills. Broadly, the internal control embedded in and over the AIS tends toward the following conditions:

- **Security routines applied at multiple levels:** The effects of focusing on security concerns, including access to programs and data, are associated with high preventive, detective, and compensating controls' costs. In brief, the virtual panopticon created by high levels of security may stifle innovation by some individuals and promote unethical avoidance schemes by others. An underappreciated aspect of ever-increasing levels of sophisticated and all-enveloping security measures is their collective effect on individuals' sense of belonging. As the prominence, potency, and prevalence of impersonal processes governed by algorithms, many of which are more dark than transparent, increases, the potential arising from individual contributions to the value chain may seem less important and unquantifiable. After all, security is not exclusively a function of capital equipment: Individual, often manual, inspection and oversight are essential for effective internal control over the AIS.

- **Flexibility demands changing unpredictably:** The effects of streamlining systems to satisfy, among other objectives, user-friendliness, and efficiency of operations are associated with ad hoc practices. Getting the task done may become a priority higher than doing it right. Control practices and standards that change too much may encourage a Wild West approach to business conduct: Anything goes, unless you are detected. Manual overrides, whether initiated at the staff, supervisory, or managerial levels, continue to pose a significant risk to the integrity of operations and quality of feedback. Training expense, among other costs, becomes a significant part of maintaining effective internal control over the AIS, making continual talent assessment a necessary compensating control for proper administration of the AIS.

- **Errors and omissions risk not accurately, completely, and timely recognized, measured, and disclosed:** See no evil; hear no evil; speak no evil is no way to conduct, inspect, and oversee one's life generally or conduct business specifically. In brief, if the technology worked as well as represented in sales puffery and public relations pieces, conduct risk would largely evaporate within the purported heat of total information awareness. However, this is rarely the case. Also, the unpredictability of errors and omissions reduces managerial effectiveness in both identifying the problem (e.g., mere error or wider fraud?) and developing the apt solution (e.g., more equipment, training, or consultants?). Estimation and assumption of the error and omission rate of both internal control and the AIS become key tasks in calibrating real effectiveness. Hype is no substitute for independent evidence of performance.

The central conflict is between natural person desire and artificial person need: Profitability and other outcomes favorable for the employer-corporation are accomplished at the expense of individuals, not all of whom prosper thereby. This is not avoidable. Production consumes resources, physical and human. The key is discovery of the actual costs and benefits, including who bears the costs and who obtains the benefits. It is in this domain that internal control and the AIS may satisfy both entities' needs and individuals' desires.

Effective control is not an ad hoc process. Rules and processes have been used by public- and private sector agencies and entities for decades. However, the advent of efficient and broad-based technological means, mostly computer based, has changed the framework for approaching internal control risks and mitigation techniques in maximization of the effectiveness of the entity's AIS: They are symbiotic in practice (see Table 4.3).

Table 4.3 Framework for control over data on assets by type

Asset data	Preventive controls	Detective controls	Compensating controls
Individuals	Limits on permissions	Continuous monitoring	Manual inspection and oversight
Funds	Segregation of duties	Daily reconciliations	Fintech of counterparty financial institutions
Other property	Centralization of authorization	Risk-based periodic audits	Inquiries of vendors and customers

The control should be directed toward the timely preparation of useful (relevant), accurate (truthful), and complete (collectively not misleading) data because the greatest risks may be too uncertain to be practicably quantifiable (namely, fraud and errors and omissions risks).

Asset data vary both in their object and in their reliability. By recognizing that internal control is what management does and requires and the AIS is what management has and uses to inform and communicate both internally and externally, the effectiveness of the integration of these tools and techniques may be understood as a complex of control systems contributing to a control environment inspected and overseen at the entity level downward. It is more vertical than horizontal; more pyramidal than flat.

The primary units of analysis are the individual and the data; these must be coordinated and controlled while adhering to the entity's mission and civil society norms, laws, and regulations. Thus, there are the following types of control activities mediating entity goals and objectives through direction and limitation of the key domains of the entity's resources (typically, individuals, funds, and other property):

- **Preventive controls:** These operate to mitigate the risk that unauthorized conduct impairs the entity's mission. Physical and logical internal control activities serve to fence in the entity's resources and restrict those without authority both from inside the entity as employees and outside the entity as agents, disclosed and undisclosed, from wreaking havoc with management's plan and the entity's proper mission. Conduct risk and asset protection are secured from wrongful, unauthorized interference initiated at all levels.
- **Detective controls:** These operate to mitigate the risk that unauthorized conduct would not be timely discovered and remediated. While some tools such as segregation of duties are longstanding, other tools such as continuous real-time monitoring have become enhanced through modern technological means, empowering widespread internal surveillance by management as an effective means of timely discovering unauthorized conduct.
- **Compensating controls:** These operate to mitigate the risk that the preventive and detective control activities would not be sufficiently and timely effective. These operate to mitigate residual risk from the hazards presented by incomplete preventive controls and inaccurate or untimely detective controls. No matter how well-thought-out a management's business plan is, there is a limit to the operating effectiveness of predefined schemes. The unforeseen or unforeseeable cannot be entirely eradicated. The real world is in flux both inside and outside of the entity; there's no substitute for hands-on inspection and oversight by supervisors, managers, officers, and directors.

As the AIS provides the inputs (i.e., accounting data and other records) that form the empirical basis for the outputs (e.g., financial statements and regulatory reports), the internal control over the processes inside and outside of the AIS supports the legitimacy, relevancy, and credibility of the entity's operational, financing, and investing functions. The inputs, processes, and outputs comprise the set of techniques otherwise known as the policies, practices, and procedures of the entity. They should be established through documentation to support the adequacy of their design, and they should be continuously tested to support the sufficiency of their implementation. Together, the AIS and management (internal) control mitigate known risks and timely confront the hazards through which unknown risks may become realized.

Though it may be unavoidable that the AIS is the primary tool through which the real world is disclosed to the entity and through which the entity presents itself to the real world (i.e., the AIS is the lens of interpretation), due care should be exercised through competent (manual) inspection and oversight techniques under the rubric of internal control. Predefined systems of control, influence, and data accumulation and analysis will ineluctably suffer from incompleteness of design. The real world may evade the AIS, demanding especially adept internal control both to recognize this contingency and to be prepared to adjust to it.

Wrap-Up (Problem Solving)

Ultimately, there are no absolute safeguards absent totalitarian imposition of control of action and information. Internal control of the AIS is ordinarily designed to provide reasonable assurance of the effectiveness of the entity's rules, processes, and data accumulation and analyses in furtherance of the entity's lawful goals and objectives consistent with civil society norms operative in the relevant jurisdiction(s). Assurance beyond reasonableness would likely bring about both high administrative costs, such as inspection and oversight, and high risk of employee and agent resistance, whether overt, such as work slowdowns, or covert, such as economic sabotage.

Control, while a necessary objective, is not without appropriate limitations. Accounting information, while essential, is not unbounded and invasive of valid expectations of privacy. To the extent successful outcomes demand socially undesirable levels of internal control and information gathering, they would force the issue of public and private priorities: Which is to be favored—personal economic gain or social respect and dignity? Are these mutually exclusive? These inquiries will not be further addressed in this chapter; however, the tensions created by the ever-growing capacity of control, exercisable through pervasive systems of surveillance and control technologies, and individual insecurity in the world (e.g., ability to satisfy basic needs without undue costs), exacerbated by displacement technologies such as artificial intelligence and machine learning, will not likely be completely mitigated any time soon.

Nonetheless, internal control should comprise the entity's rules and processes designed to assure that evidence-based inputs are timely converted into actionable facts, allowing both the articulation of economic reality through accounting and corroborating data and the accountability of management, staff, and agents measured against the accomplishment of the proper goals and objectives of the entity.

While the focus of this chapter has been on the relationship between internal control and AISs, a concern that superficially would not include a deep and wide study of macro-level effects, there are civil society and regulatory movements (e.g., individual privacy rights) impacting data accumulation and use afoot that are relevant to global enterprises, especially those with a nexus to the European Union (European Commission's General Data Protection Regulation 2016/679 updated 2018).

Presently, the most prominent issues facing internal control and the AIS are individual privacy rights and corporate cybersecurity obligations. These may operate at cross-purposes: For example, an individual's right to control his or her personally sensitive data may be seen to conflict with an entity's obligation to safeguard these data. In the domain of exchange transactions, key data are transferred to and from counterparties, and in the domain of regulation, key data are transferred to and from the regulators. The rules and processes affecting these data are not without unquantifiable error and omission both in design and implementation. Individuals often lose exclusive protection, custody, and control over their personally sensitive (and other) data for security purposes, whether national or corporate in scope.

There is no substitute for managerial competence in preparation of reports based directly or indirectly on AISs and on ensuring reasonable assurance of the underlying accounting and corroborative data through an effective system of internal control. As noted by Abraham Briloff (2004):

we find our first rate accounting scholars carrying on their research as second rate finance–economic scholars, e.g., the efficient market, working with third rate mathematical models, programmed with fourth rate aggregate data, culled from fifth rate databanks, compiled by sixth rate crones. (p. 790)

The Briloff message may be readily inverted and extended from the domain of academic research into the real world of entities and enterprises, whether for-profit, not-for-profit, or governmental. AIS provides the conceptual framework of generally relevant data, which are specfically determined by the entity's venues, jurisdictions, and business plans. Internal control is collectively the policy, practices, and procedures enforcement arm of the entity operating under the goals of accomplishing, maintaining, and remediating, where necessary, the condition of possession of high-quality data that provides timely and relevant feedback of the entity itself. If data are not carefully accumulated and analyzed, and internal control is neglected in design or implementation, the likely medium- and long-term survival of the entity is at risk.

Perhaps most importantly, entities should maintain adequate diligence over the finance, technology, and engineering fields relevant to their operations and civil society at large. These key industries provide management with tools and incentives to control individual discretion consistent with entity goals and objectives The respective states of the art may counsel for enhanced mathematical and physical techniques to limit dissemination of data and dampen conduct risk, but ethical and farseeing management should recognize that validity of data is not equivalent to soundness of data. That is, the data may be consistent within the rules and processes developed in-house or purchased from any one of a number of people-analytics and employee monitoring for-profit vendors, but the data may be false and misleading (e.g., characterized by fraud in valuation of transactions and accounts): The audit trail may be internally consistent but factually bogus.

However, with the substantial assistance of the financial, technology, and engineering industries, accurate, complete, and timely information regarding employees and agents for use in a continuously monitored and audited control environment inspected and overseen by directors and officers as necessary is feasible as never before.

- **Financial:** Records and reports regarding operating and capital transactions of the entity and its counterparties may readily be inputted and analyzed. The initiation, authorization, execution, and feedback related to these transactions may be examined and reexamined as required. Reliable feedback, including through financial, performance, and compliance audits, is timely available.
- **Technology:** The capacity of management to monitor in real time not only the preparation and processing of data from records but the mitigation of conduct risk through people-analytics tools and techniques generating virtual and empirical awareness evidence is greater than previously imaginable. Scientific management is more than an ideal; it is a real alternative and not just for factories.
- **Engineering:** Physical and logical means to detect, prevent, and compensate for substandard employee and agent performance is more affordable and effective than ever before. Entities may develop their own protective and detective methods to limit employee and agent discretion throughout their chain of command, whether horizontal or vertical. Vendors and consultants are globally available to assist management in the design, implementation, and maintenance of appropriate control systems.

The tools and techniques available to management, including powerful AISs, for exercising proper control over the employees, agents, and assets under its stewardship are vast. However, these tools and techniques do not and should not operate outside of civil society and the rule of law. Management should apply due care in the use of control activities lest blowback occur. Overly controlled natural persons may rebel; adverse conditions such as mental or physical health impairments may follow. The extent to which entities externalize these adversities may provide a temporary respite, but medium- and long-term solutions demand more than cost and obligation shifting to other sectors within civil society. "No man is an island entire of itself" (Donne 1624). Analogously, no enterprise or entity will long survive antipathy from the civil society within which it is embedded. Values such as privacy count, too.

CHAPTER 5

Accounting Information Systems and the U.S. Health Care Industry

David M. Shapiro

Introduction and Overview

According to the North American Industry Classification System (NAICS) manual published in 2017 by the U.S. Office of Management and Budget (OMB), health care and social assistance should be grouped together (namely, sector 62) because of their commonalities and unclear boundaries between them (see U.S. OMB 2017). Fundamentally, sector 62 circumscribes services (i.e., labor inputs) typically delivered by health practitioners to individuals. Due to the nature of health care delivered, financed, and charged for in the United States, the accounting information system (AIS) is first and foremost used to identify the nature of these health practitioner labor inputs and quantify their monetary values for the purpose of calculating costs, expenses, losses, and revenues. Similarly, the AIS should account for the consumption of supplies and cost recovery of capital expenditures. The financial interests of the individual patients, the health practitioners, and third-party payers, such as for-profit (investor-owned) insurance plans, nonprofit hospitals, and public sector assistance agencies and programs (e.g., Medicare, Tricare, Medicaid), among others, demand accurate, complete, and timely recognition, measurement, and disclosure of these costs and expenses, whether reimbursable or not reimbursable to the given entity or individual. In brief, there are two key financial interests invoking the utility and robustness of the entity's AIS: value of profit or surplus and obligation or right of reimbursement. These financial interests are defined and controlled through effective coding, predefined and discretionary, facilitated by the AIS.

The U.S. health care system is both market based and government subsidized at the individual and practitioner levels or units of analysis. Intermediation by third-party administrators in the private and public sectors such as health insurance plans exerts a significant influence over these units of analysis; that is, often, individuals seek to cover health insurance costs through these third parties, and practitioners seek to support their revenues through payments by these third parties. According to the U.S. Centers for Medicare and Medicaid Services (CMS), national health expenditures in the United States for 2016 were $10,348 per individual, accounting for 17.9 percent of gross domestic product (GDP) (see U.S. CMS 2016). The U.S. health care industry is both large from the accounting, financial, and economic perspectives and significant from the mortality, morbidity, and quality of life perspectives. Without denigrating the importance of the latter perspectives, this chapter is more directly and immediately focused on the former perspectives, which more or less incorporate the latter perspectives through assessment of health care treatment outcomes that bear on practitioner payments authorized by third-party payers and administrators; that is, health care payments may be founded in part on the effectiveness of the health care services for the benefit of the individual patient. Thereby, quality of care may impact practitioner revenue and cash collections.

Accounting for this naturally complex and artificially complicated system requires a robust AIS that maintains interoperability with third-party payer and administrators' requirements. Standardization and uniformity are essential attributes for the AIS to serve as an effective means of preparing and supporting practitioner and individuals' claims. This chapter focuses on practitioner requirements in relation to third-party payers and administrators as few patients have the wherewithal, including time, money, and incentives, to commit to the purchase or development of their own customized AIS. Without an effective AIS, the practitioner is likely fated to deficiencies in cash collections, including a lack of timely payments by third parties.

While accuracy, completeness, and timeliness are essential attributes of an AIS, especially with respect to the preparation of invoices, claims, and other statements supporting the provision and valuation of health care services, fraud and abuse have not been eradicated as significant risks in the U.S. health care industry, notwithstanding enhanced and powerful AISs. According to the U.S. Department of Health and Human Services Health Care Fraud and Abuse Control Annual Report for fiscal year 2017, the U.S. government alone negotiated or won over $2.4 billion in health care fraud settlements and judgments during fiscal year 2017 (see U.S. HHS 2017); this figure excludes state settlements and judgments implicating, among other legal causes of actions, litigation arising from defrauding state Medicaid programs.

Fraud as an intentional misrepresentation of health care services offered and their proper valuation is only one concern of managerial inspection and oversight of the AIS: Unintentional under- and overbilling are also legitimate concerns. The accuracy and completeness of the expenditure, cost recovery, and revenue processes are also at issue. However, as the U.S. health care industry is characterized by extensive use of intermediation such as private health care plans and government health care programs that come between the individual patient and the health care practitioner to administer and finance the delivery of health care, there is significant opportunity for fraud: The payer is removed from the recipient of care and the provider of care. This removal and distance facilitate deception; the patient cannot realistically check the performance and billing of the practitioner, and he or she does not have the incentive to do so beyond certain thresholds such as deductibles.

The opportunity structure of the U.S. health care industry readily allows fraud notwithstanding the most robust and efficient of AISs, which is not to suggest that the AIS is anything but the linchpin of the health care system from the financial perspective (see Table 5.1). As usual, the

Table 5.1 Opportunity structure of U.S. health care industry

Domain	Inputs (e.g., labor)	Process (e.g., AIS)	Output (e.g., billings)
Patient	Uninformed	Alienated	Intimidated
Practitioner	Initiation hazard	Technical preparation	Overreach hazard
Intermediary	Authorization hazard	Technical edits	Underreach hazard

actions of corrupt management override and unethical or illicit discretionary conduct at other levels may cause the AIS to prepare and issue materially misleading claims, invoices, statements, and reports.

There are problems within each domain that facilitate the occurrence, filing, and concealment of fraudulent acts and false reports, including the following:

- Patients are especially vulnerable, usually lacking expertise over the medical diagnoses and prognoses and effectiveness of treatment protocols and procedures. Patients are largely uninformed about their condition, how to treat it, what drugs, if any, should be prescribed, and so on; that is, the asymmetry of information between the patient and the practitioner and intermediary is practicably unreconcilable. While some patients may become somewhat informed through research, the medical jargon and billing codes are exceedingly complex and complicated. The distinctions between natural complexity evident in diseases such as cancer and artificial complications evident in design science structures such as billing codes for medical procedures and treatments are important to consider: Complexity may be irreducible in many respects; complicated designs are by-products of an inefficient system that may be mitigated through intelligent transformation. Patients may be predisposed to accept expert practitioner or authoritative administrator opinions (e.g., they may fail to challenge denials of claims).

- Practitioners are generally more expert in their chosen field (e.g., oncology) than in the discipline of database management or design science (e.g., medical billing software). Compliance with AIS coding requirements may be outsourced or managed within the practice, though the practitioner would ordinarily be responsible for the accuracy and completeness of the billings. While many subfields within the health care industry in the United States are lucrative and would superficially seem to be beyond the need for practitioner-inspired cheating, they also offer profit-making opportunities that patients cannot often meaningfully check or practicably control. Practitioners may be biased to maximize inflows of financial resources (e.g., inflating the value of their claims of third-party payers).

- Intermediaries, including third-party payers, are also besieged by the same artificial complications arising both at the macro level (e.g., federal regulations and rules governing Medicare) and the meso level (e.g., hair-splitting coding to distinguish coverages and rates applicable to numerous medical procedures and courses of treatment). These inherently technical and jargonized design systems are made more vulnerable to errors, omissions, and fraud where they intersect with potential profit-making incentives at these intermediaries. Health insurance plans have a financial motivation to control their loss ratios (e.g., what is paid as a valid claim). Also, neither not-for-profit organizations nor public sector programs can credibly assert to be unconcerned and impartial to the conservation of financial resources. Intermediaries may be biased to minimize outflows of financial resources (e.g., paying claims of practitioners or patients).

While there is no doubt as to the present size and importance of the U.S. health care industry, due care would demand that recognition be made of the industry's dependence on both technology and government policy.

Special Accounting and Financial Reporting Issues

Among the key revenue and expense AIS issues with which the U.S. health care industry should become familiar are the following (see Granof et al. 2015):

- Conformance with requests for reimbursement reporting under the diagnosis-related groups' (DRGs) conceptual framework of Medicare's prospective payment system for patient service revenues;
- Computation of estimated contractual adjustments where contractual patient service revenue rates are discounted;
- Computation of estimated bad debts expense, especially where revenue collections directly from patients may be reliably extrapolated from historical records of nonpayment;
- Computation of the indirect and direct costs of providing charity care services (where no cash inflows are expected);

- Recognition and measurement of capitation fee revenues under agreements to provide health care (separate and apart from actually providing health care services);
- Computation of estimated loss contingencies (e.g., malpractice claims where both the liability has been incurred and the amount of loss is reasonably estimable);
- Computation of retrospective insurance premiums, especially where claims against the insured are greater than expected and subject to retrospective adjustment by the insurer.

These performance indicators apply directly or indirectly to for-profit, not-for-profit, and governmental health care entities. Reconciliation between cash flows and the full accrual basis demands an AIS that holds detailed relevant historical records of agreements and transactions with numerous counterparties, including patients, practitioners, and intermediaries in the private and public sectors. Moreover, estimates of items such as contractual adjustments and bad debts require attention to emerging trends in the health care industry, including regulation at the federal and state levels, such that maintaining and enhancing the AIS under changing attendant circumstances are routine, efficient, and effective.

Skilled managerial inspection and oversight should be applied to modern software applications. This is especially necessary in the complex web of patient claims and practitioner and third-party intermediary costs and revenues that offer opportunity, incentive, and pressures to submit erroneous or fraudulent data. Without the proficient and panoptic inspector and overseer, the hazardous terrain of the U.S. health care system may permit too much of the worst kinds of unfavorable outcomes: inflated costs and poor health maintenance.

Special Hazards and Risks

The AIS is a technological solution to problems inherent in the administration of often complex diagnoses and courses of treatment of patients by practitioners under the complicated regulatory regimes of intermediaries. The applicability and amount of third-party payer coverage looms large as a significant factor in the decision making of individuals across the domains of patient, practitioner, and intermediary. In the U.S. health care industry, design science like that which produced the AIS meets the natural sciences implicated in medical issues, including biology and chemistry. The asymmetries of information among suffering patient, treating practitioner, and third-party administration (TPA) are daunting. Even assuming that the AISs between practitioner and TPA reflect each other fairly accurately and comprehensively, the patient cannot independently and intelligently check the inputs, processes, and outputs of these party and counterparty AIS. The roots of these difficulties may be approached using the outline identified in Table 5.2.

Table 5.2 Risk assessment and language at key levels in the U.S. health care industry

Language	Patients	Practitioners	Intermediaries
Natural—common	Low	Medium	High
Technical—medical	High	Low	Medium
Technical—accounting	Medium	Low	Medium

These broadly applied assessments of risk arising from each indicated and generalized hazard are not intended to depict with mathematical accuracy or precision the levels of difficulty that patients, practitioners, and intermediaries experience with the U.S. health care system. Instead, Table 5.2 is intended to provoke creative thinking and problem-solving skills in the concerned reader. In brief, the descriptions of disease used by patients are transformed into artificial classifications used by practitioners and intermediaries to govern recoverability of costs under whatever courses of medical or health care treatment are delivered: The language of the ill and diseased confronts the languages of cost accounting and medical bureaucracy, resulting in an expensive or profitable (depending on one's perspective) labyrinthine structuring of delivery and financing of health care services of variable effectiveness.

The plight and informational resources of the buyers (broadly, the patients) are dwarfed by the position and resources of the sellers (broadly, the practitioners). For better and worse, intermediaries such as third-party administrators are caught between the buyers and sellers in a regulatory web of accounting for health care services and financing (or not) their delivery. The AIS mediates between the provision of the service and the recovery of cost (with an implicit rate of return).

Wrap-Up (Problem Solving)

The opportunity structure of the U.S. health care industry may, without much exaggeration, be described as criminogenic (see the NHCAA 2018), vulnerabilities that allow illicit exploitation resulting in financial crimes by white-collar criminals. There are numerous methods available to practitioners to scam third-party payers and patients alike, and this should not be interpreted as a whitewash of criminogenic potentiality in patients and intermediaries. Credible research points toward the unfortunate effects of rising costs and limited access to health care in the United States (see Austin and Hungerford 2010).

In fact and by operation of law, the U.S. health care system poses threats that should be managed through coordination at the federal, state, and local law enforcement agency levels (see U.S. Attorneys' Manual 1998). Thus, patients, practitioners, and intermediaries are impacted by audits and investigations arising across the law enforcement agency spectrum, including sanctions resulting from criminal, civil, and administrative proceedings. This demands a highly accountable, transparent, and effective AIS in support of health care expenditures and claims derived therefrom. However, the AIS as an essential tool under management may be misused or abused notwithstanding laws and regulations prohibiting wrongful conduct through criminal, civil, and administrative proceedings. Moreover, the potential inspection and oversight by law enforcement agencies coordinated across federal, state, and local levels imposes a significant informational and compliance demand on the target's AIS. There is high inherent legal and business risk to operating in the U.S. health care industry: Fraud is tempting yet discoverable.

An opportunity structure such as the U.S. health care system needs robust and impartial inspection and oversight to supplement a well-crafted system of rule of law. In many material respects, the United States has neither of these key mediator variables necessary to mitigate conduct risk to a tolerably low level. That the U.S. health care system is more competition between practitioners and intermediaries to obtain and allocate financial resources under the language of provision of health care services and courses of treatment than a cooperative venture among practitioners, intermediaries, and patients to impact favorably and improve cost-effectively patient outcomes, namely their health and welfare, is fairly clear.

Notwithstanding some valuable suggestions about improving the health care system more around the margins than at its incentivized, for-profit (investor-owned, directed, and controlled) core such as value-based health care strategy (see Porter and Lee 2013), designing, implementing, maintaining, and, where necessary, improving the AIS tool and management's techniques in using this tool need to fit within the control (or lack of control) environment as it is and not as it should be. This suggests voluntarily adopting (or involuntarily requiring) the sustained application of the following procedures:

- Design and implement the AIS in recognition of the principle of sufficient reason; that is, the AIS may not represent facts but only what has been inputted as evidence. Thus, rigorous and intelligent review and approval at the transaction and account levels are essential. Fraud and material omissions are serious risks especially pertinent to the U.S. health care system.

- Consider the fraud risk resulting from the moral hazard of cross-purposes: Performance indicators prioritizing profit-making may not adequately serve patient health and welfare outcomes. Thus, an internal audit unit or similarly functioning and adequately staffed group reporting to officers and directors should exercise rigorous risk-based inspection and oversight of the reporting entity beyond the bottom line. This demands more than lip service: Competent staffing and sufficient resources are key to prevent and detect fraudulent or misleadingly erroneous reporting.

- Consider the potentiality of an automated panopticon control mechanism by which transactions and balances are subjected to inspection and oversight effectuated largely without managerial discretion. Issues such as initiation and authorization of transactions would require inputs from patient, practitioner, and third-party intermediary, resulting in a blockchain-type (i.e., a peer-to-peer-to-peer, electronically created and maintained ledger) account and transaction structure. Expansion of meaningful inspection and oversight is essential for civil society and the general welfare.

- Assess and mitigate the risks accompanying the application of statistical methods to test transactions and account balances. Fundamentally, there are three types of outcomes: (1) the false positive by which an event is erroneously flagged, thereby wasting resources in its ultimate validation; (2) the false negative by which an event is erroneously treated as valid, thereby increasing the risk that the entity faces, among other things, criminal, civil, or administrative sanctions; (3) the accurate conclusion that the event according to both the AIS and objective reality reasonably and materially agrees.

- Invoice information and communication should be accompanied by detailed, meaningful, and readily understandable plain English corroborating documentation. The inability of the patient to check the data within an invoice that is prepared more for the benefit of communication in acceptable code to third-party payers like insurance companies and public sector health plans than for empowering the patient to act as a fraud and error detective control contributes to runaway and wrongful patient costs and inflated and misleading practitioner or intermediary revenues.

- Practitioner procedures should be organized into project and budget format, empowering all of the key participants to make informed assumptions and intelligent estimates about the expected costs (and revenues) of health care delivery units, whether services such as surgeries or goods such as pharmaceuticals. Thus, the AIS should be fairly standardized and uniform across practitioners and intermediaries to promote the practice of responsible decision making by patients, most of whom are not adequately informed about the likely costs of their course of care. The unit of analysis for AIS evaluation is not merely the reporting entity but civil society, especially the patient, at large.

The ability to succeed and report successful outcomes in the U.S. health care industry is in large part a managerial and operational problem;

that is, patients, practitioners, intermediaries, and regulators require that specific rules, processes, and data be inspected and overseen from bottom-to-top and top-to-bottom directions. The AIS is management's essential tool by which it accurately and completely records and processes data according to the rules of accountability that may not adequately control for conflicts of interest and incentives (e.g., more financial profit at the practitioner level may be correlated with less appropriate care at the patient level).

Moreover, the asymmetry of information among the key participant groups in the industry results in a control system not characterized by effective checks and balances among these groups at the macro level; that is, there is no widely practiced and comprehensive inspection and oversight regime within and across the American states. For example, the State of Kansas's Legislative Division of Post Audit's performance report on privatization of the state's Medicaid program indicated significant data reliability problems among patients' claims, practitioners' services, and health care outcomes datasets (State of Kansas LDPA 2018).

Health care expenditures are abnormally high in the short- and medium terms and not sustainable in the long term. These circumstances may result in the practical necessity for the design and implementation of AISs in the United States that are less focused on reporting entity profitability and more focused on patient health outcomes, while preserving patient confidentiality and related cybersecurity objectives. Therefore, even a collaborative AIS scheme among patient, practitioner, and third-party intermediary would pose a significant risk of failure to protect the patient absent significant public or third-party inspection and oversight (see Kaminski 2018).

In light of the available computer-based technology, which enhances both the preparation of accounting information and health care outcome metrics, the potential improvement of the U.S. health care system is readily imaginable notwithstanding the risks of fraud and error inherent in the current regime. Political will and courage may be necessary to wrap a benevolent and uniform social fabric around profit-seeking and not-for-profit institutions to enhance the general welfare, a civil society goal that should not be hollowed out by institutional missions and objectives detached from its furtherance.

Bibliography

Abbasi, A., C. Albrecht, A. Vance, and J. Hansen. 2012. "MetaFraud: A Meta-learning Framework for Detecting Financial Fraud." *MIS Quarterly* 36, no. 4, pp. 1293–1327. http://ez.lib.jjay.cuny.edu/login?url=http://search.ebscohost.com/login.aspx?direct=true&db=bth&AN=83465956&site=ehost-live, (accessed January 26, 2018).

Abdel-Rahim, H.Y., and D.E. Stevens. 2018. "Information System Precision and Honesty in Managerial Reporting: A Re-examination of Information Asymmetry Effects." *Accounting, Organizations and Society* 64, pp. 31–43. doi:10.1016/j.aos.2017.12.004.

Accounting Information Systems. 2013. http://www.accountinginformationsystems.org/, (accessed January 24, 2018).

Ai, L., and J. Tang. 2011. "Risk-based Approach for Designing Enterprise-wide AML Information System Solution." *Journal of Financial Crime* 18, no. 3, pp. 268–76. doi:10.1108/13590791111147488.

AICPA (American Institute of Public Accountants). 2019. "Competency and Learning." https://competency.aicpa.org/.

Akerlof, G.A., P.M. Romer, R.E. Hall, and N.G. Mankiw. 1993. "Looting: The Economic Underworld of Bankruptcy for Profit." *Brookings Papers on Economic Activity* 1993, no. 2, pp. 1–73. doi:10.2307/2534564.

Austin, A.D., and T.L. Hungerford. May 25, 2010. "The Market Structure of the Health Insurance Industry," *Congressional Research Service.* https://fas.org/sgp/crs/misc/R40834.pdf, (accessed June 8, 2018).

Axelos. 2019. "What is ITIL Best Practice?" https://www.axelos.com/best-practice-solutions/itil/what-is-itil.

Baader, G., and H. Krcmar. 2018. "Reducing False Positives in Fraud Detection: Combining the Red Flag Approach with Process Mining." *International Journal of Accounting Information Systems* 31, pp. 1–16.

Baker, C.R., B. Cohanier, and N.J. Leo. 2017. "Breakdowns in Internal Controls in Bank Trading Information Systems: The Case of the Fraud at Société Générale." *International Journal of Accounting Information Systems* 26, pp. 20–31. doi:10.1016/j.accinf.2017.06.002.

Bhattacherjee, A., and U. Shrivastava. 2018. "The Effects of ICT Use and ICT Laws on Corruption: A General Deterrence Theory Perspective." *Government Information Quarterly* 35, no. 4, pp. 703–712.

Bierstaker, J.L., D. Hanes-Downey, J.M. Rose, and J.C. Thibodeau. 2018. "Effects of Stories and Checklist Decision Aids on Knowledge Structure Development and Auditor Judgment." *Journal of Information Systems* 32, no. 2, pp. 1–24. doi:10.2308/isys-51913.

Black, W.K. 2011. "Neo-Classical Economic Theories, Methodology, and Praxis Optimize Criminogenic Environments and Produce Recurrent, Intensifying Crises." *Creighton Law Review* 44, no. 3, pp. 597–645. http://search.ebscohost.com.ez.lib.jjay.cuny.edu/login.aspx?direct=true&db=a9h&AN=60908120&site=ehost-live.

Bluth, R. June 20, 2019. "1 in 6 Insured Hospital Patients Get a Surprise Bill for Out-of-Network Care," *Kaiser Health News*. https://khn.org/news/1-in-6-insured-hospital-patients-get-a-surprise-bill-for-out-of-network-care/.

Brazel, J.F., K.L. Jones, and D.F. Prawitt. 2014. "Auditors' Reactions to Inconsistencies between Financial and Nonfinancial Measures: The Interactive Effects of Fraud Risk Assessment and a Decision Prompt." *Behavioral Research in Accounting* 26, no.1, pp. 131–56. doi:10.2308/bria-50630.

Briloff, A. 2004. "Accounting scholars in the groves of academe In Pari Delicto." *Critical Perspectives on Accounting* 15, no. 6–7, pp. 787–96. doi:10.1016/j.cpa.2003.03.002.

Briloff, A.J. 2001. "Garbage In/Garbage Out: A Critique of Fraudulent Financial Reporting: 1987–1997 (the COSO Report) and The SEC Accounting Regulatory Process." *Critical Perspectives on Accounting* 12, no. 2, pp. 125–48. doi:10.1006/cpac.2001.0458.

Casselman, B. April 25, 2018. "What Amazon's New Headquarters Could Mean for Rents," *The New York Times*. https://www.nytimes.com/2018/04/25/business/economy/amazon-hq-rents.html, (accessed April 27, 2018).

Chang, S.-I., D.C. Yen, C.S.-P. Ng, I.-C. Chang, and S.-Y. Yu. 2011. "An ERP System Performance Assessment Model Development Based on the Balanced Scorecard Approach (Report)." *Information Systems Frontiers* 13, no. 3, pp. 429–50. doi:10.1007/s10796-009-9225-5.

Chartered Global Management Accountant. n.d. "Become a CGMA." https://www.cgma.org/becomeacgma.html, (accessed January 27, 2018).

CIMA (Chartered Institute of Management Accountants). 2019. "CIMA Qualifications Framework." https://www.cimaglobal.com/Qualifications/Syllabus/.

Committee of Sponsoring Organizations of the Treadway Commission. 2019. "Guidance." https://www.coso.org/Pages/guidance.aspx.

Comptroller General of the United States. 2011. "Government Auditing Standards." https://www.gao.gov/assets/590/587281.pdf, (accessed May 21, 2018).

De Korvin, A., M.F. Shipley, and K. Omer. 2004. "Assessing Risks Due to Threats to Internal Control in a Computer-Based Accounting Information System: A Pragmatic Approach Based on Fuzzy Set Theory." *Intelligent Systems in Accounting, Finance & Management* 12, no. 2, pp. 139–52. doi:10.1002/isaf.249.

Dilla, W.N., A.J. Harrison, B.E. Mennecke, and D.J. Janvrin. 2013. "The Assets Are Virtual but the Behavior Is Real: An Analysis of Fraud in Virtual Worlds and Its Implications for the Real World." *Journal of Information Systems* 27, no. 2, pp. 131–58. doi:10.2308/isys-50571.

Djalil, M., S.E. Nadirsyah, M.R. Yahya, J. Jalaluddin, and S.V. Ramadhanti. 2017. "The Effect of Used Information Technology, Internal Control, and Regional Accounting System on the Performance of City Governance Agency of Banda Aceh City, Indonesia." *Brand Research in Accounting* 8, no. 1, pp. 25–37. https://doaj.org/article/361953fdeae14251a303657fcecd979f, (accessed May 11, 2018).

Donne, J. 1624. "Devotions upon Emergent Occasions, Meditation XVII," *Wikisource*. https://en.wikisource.org/wiki/Meditation_XVII, (accessed June 5, 2018).

Durney, M., R. Elder, and S. Glover. 2014. "Field Data on Accounting Error Rates and Audit Sampling." *Auditing* 33, no. 2, pp. 79–110.

Edin, P.A., T. Evans, G. Graetz, S. Hernnas, and G. Michaels. June 24, 2019. "The Individual Consequences of Occupational Decline," *VOX*. https://voxeu.org/article/individual-consequences-occupational-decline.

Eldenburg, L., N. Soderstrom, V. Willis, and A. Wu. 2010. "Behavioral Changes Following the Collaborative Development of an Accounting Information System." *Accounting, Organizations and Society* 35, no. 2, pp. 222–37. doi:10.1016/j.aos.2009.07.005.

European Commission. 2018. "2018 Reform of EU Data Protection Rules." https://ec.europa.eu/commission/priorities/justice-and-fundamental-rights/data-protection/2018-reform-eu-data-protection-rules_en, (accessed May 26, 2018).

FBI. 2018. "Internet Crime Report." https://www.ic3.gov/media/annual-report/2018_IC3Report.pdf.

Flowerday, S., A.W. Blundell, and R. Von Solms. July 2006. "Continuous Auditing Technologies and Models: A Discussion." *Computers & Security* 25, no. 5, pp. 325–31. doi:10.1016/j.cose.2006.06.004.

Geerts, G.L., W.E. McCarthy, and S.R. Rockwell. 1996. "Automated Integration of Enterprise Accounting Models Throughout the Systems Development Life Cycle." *Intelligent Systems in Accounting, Finance & Management* 5, no. 3, pp. 113–28.

Ghasemi, M., V. Shafeiepour, M. Aslani, and E. Barvayeh. 2011. "The impact of Information Technology (IT) on modern accounting systems." *Procedia - Social and Behavioral Sciences* 28, pp. 112–16. doi:10.1016/j.sbspro.2011.11.023.

Granof, M., S.B. Khumawala, T.D. Calabrese, and D.L. Smith. 2015. *Government and Not-for-Profit Accounting Concepts and Practices.* 7th ed. New York, NY: Wiley.

Hansson, S.O. 2018. "Risk." In *The Stanford Encyclopedia of Philosophy* (Fall 2018 Edition), ed. Edward N. Zalta. https://plato.stanford.edu/archives/fall2018/entries/risk/.

Hao, K. May 31, 2019. "The AI Gig Economy is Coming for You," *MIT Technology Review.* https://www.technologyreview.com/s/613606/the-ai-gig-economy-is-coming-for-you/.

Haynes, R., and C. Li. 2016. "Continuous Audit and Enterprise Resource Planning Systems: A Case Study of ERP Rollouts in the Houston, TX Oil and Gas Industries." *Journal of Emerging Technologies in Accounting* 13, no. 1, pp. 171–79. doi:10.2308/jeta-51446.

Hunton, J. 2002. "Blending Information and Communication Technology with Accounting Research." *Accounting Horizons* 16, no. 1, pp. 55–67.

IMA (Institute of Management Accountant). 2019. "The CMA." https://www.imanet.org/cma-certification-lp/global?utm_source=bing&utm_medium=cpc&utm_campaign=(CMA)%20Brand%20HeadTerms&utm_term=institute%20of%20management%20accountants&utm_content=IMA%20Brand%20-%20Head%20Term&ssopc=1.

ISACA (Information Systems Audit and Control Association). 2019. "About ISACA." http://www.isaca.org/about-isaca/Pages/default.aspx.

ISACA. 2018. "Certified Information Systems Auditor." http://www.isaca .org/Certification/CISA-Certified-Information-Systems-Auditor/ Pages/default.aspx, (accessed March 26, 2018).

Institute of Internal Auditors. 2017. "International Standards for the Professional Practice of Internal Auditing (Standards)." https://na.theiia.org/ standards-guidance/Public%20Documents/IPPF-Standards-2017.pdf, (accessed May 12, 2018).

International Association of Privacy Professionals. 2018. "About the IAPP." https://iapp.org/about/, (accessed March 26, 2013).

International Auditing and Assurance Standards Board. 2016–2017. "Handbook of International Quality Control, Auditing, Review, Other Assurance, and Related Services Pronouncements." https://www .ifac.org/publications-resources/2016-2017-handbook-international- quality-control-auditing-review-other, (accessed May 13, 2018).

International Federation of Accountants, International Accounting Education Standards Board. 2018. "Information and Communications Technology Literature Review." https://www.ifac.org/publications- resources/information-and-communications-technology-literature- review, (accessed April 16, 2018).

(ISC)². 2019. "(ISC)²: The World's Leading Cybersecurity and IT Security Professional Organization." https://www.isc2.org/About, (accessed January 27, 2018).

ISO. n.d. "Management System Standards." https://www.iso.org/ management-system-standards.html.

Japan Times. n.d. "Toshiba Accounting Scandal." https://www.japantimes .co.jp/tag/toshiba-accounting-scandal/, (accessed January 29, 2018).

Kaminski, M.E. June 15, 2018. "The Right to Explanation, Explained." https://ssrn.com/abstract=3196985, (accessed June 20, 2018).

Kim, R., J. Gangolly, and P. Elsas. 2017. "A Framework for Analytics and Simulation of Accounting Information Systems: A Petri Net Modeling Primer." *International Journal of Accounting Information Systems* 27, pp. 30–54. doi:10.1016/j.accinf.2017.09.002.

Kotb, A., C. Roberts, and S. Sian. 2012. "E-business Audit: Advisory Jurisdiction or Occupational Invasion?" *Critical Perspectives on Accounting* 23, no. 6, pp. 468–82. doi:10.1016/j.cpa.2012.03.003.

Lehman, C.R., and F. Okcabol. 2005. "Accounting for Crime." *Critical Perspectives on Accounting* 16, no. 5, pp. 613–39. doi:10.1016/j.cpa.2003.08.003.

Li, C., G.F. Peters, V.J. Richardson, and M.W. Watson. 2012. "The Consequences of Information Technology Control Weaknesses on Management Information Systems: The Case of Sarbanes-Oxley Internal Control Reports." *MIS Quarterly* 36, no. 1, pp. 179–203. http://www.jstor.org/stable/41410413, (accessed March 28, 2018).

Li, C., G.F. Peters, V.J. Richardson, and M.W. Watson. 2012. "The Consequences of Information Technology Control Weaknesses on Management Information Systems: The Case of Sarbanes-Oxley Internal Control Reports." *MIS Quarterly* 36, no. 1, p. 179. http://www.jstor.org.ez.lib.jjay.cuny.edu/stable/41410413, (accessed May 11, 2018).

Li, H., J. Dai, T. Gershberg, and M.A. Vasarhelyi. 2018. "Understanding Usage and Value of Audit Analytics for Internal Auditors: An Organizational Approach." *International Journal of Accounting Information Systems* 28, pp. 59–76. doi:10.1016/j.accinf.2017.12.005.

Liu, C., L.J. Yao, C.L. Sia, and K.K. Wei. 2014. "The Impact of Early XBRL Adoption on Analysts' Forecast Accuracy—Empirical Evidence from China." *Electronic Markets* 24, no. 1, pp. 47–55. doi:10.1007/s12525-013-0132-8, (accessed April 11, 2018).

Lombardi, D.R., and R.B. Dull. 2016. "The Development of AudEx: An Audit Data Assessment System." *Journal of Emerging Technologies in Accounting* 13, no. 1, pp. 37–52. doi:10.2308/jeta-51445.

McLaren, J., T. Appleyard, and F. Mitchell. 2016. "The Rise and Fall of Management Accounting Systems: A Case Study Investigation of EVA™." *The British Accounting Review* 48, no. 3, pp. 341–58. doi:10.1016/j.bar.2016.02.001.

Mock, T.J., R.P. Srivastava, and A.M. Wright. 2017. "Fraud Risk Assessment Using the Fraud Risk Model as a Decision Aid." *Journal of Emerging Technologies in Accounting* 14, no. 1, pp. 37–56. doi:10.2308/jeta-51724.

Mu, E., L.J. Kirsch, and B.S. Butler. 2015. "The Assimilation of Enterprise Information System: An Interpretation Systems Perspective." *Information & Management* 52, no. 3, pp. 359–70. doi:10.1016/j.im.2015.01.004.

NHCAA (National Health Care Anti-Fraud Association). 2018. "The Challenge of Health Care Fraud." https://www.nhcaa.org/resources/ health-care-anti-fraud-resources/the-challenge-of-health-care-fraud .aspx, (accessed June 8, 2018).

Nissan, E. 2013. "Legal Evidence and Advanced Computing Techniques for Combatting Crime: An Overview." *Information & Communications Technology Law* 22, no. 3, pp. 1–38.

NIST. n.d. "Topics." https://www.nist.gov/topics.

O'Donnell, D., N. Bontis, P. O'Regan, T. Kennedy, P. Cleary, and A. Hannigan. 2004. "CFOs in E-business: E-architects or Foot-soldiers?" *Knowledge and Process Management* 11, no. 2, pp. 105–116. doi:10 .1002/kpm.196, (accessed April 11, 2018).

PCAOB (Public Company Accounting and Oversight Board). 2019. "Standards." https://pcaobus.org/standards.

PCAOB. 2017. "Auditing Standards of the Public Company Accounting Oversight Board." https://pcaobus.org/Standards/Auditing/Documents/ PCAOB_Auditing_Standards_as_of_December_15_2017.pdf, (accessed May 13, 2018).

Porter, M.E., and T.H. Lee. October 2013. "The Strategy That Will Fix Health Care," *Harvard Business Review*. https://hbr.org/2013/10/the-strategy-that-will-fix-health-care, (accessed June 8, 2018).

Poston, R.S., and S.V. Grabski. 2000. "Accounting Information Systems Research: Is it Another QWERTY?" *International Journal of Accounting Information Systems* 1, no. 1, pp. 9–53. doi:10.1016/S1467-0895 (99)00003-2.

Prechel, H., and L. Zheng. 2016. "Do Organizational and Political–Legal Arrangements Explain Financial Wrongdoing?" *The British Journal of Sociology* 67, pp. 655–77. doi:10.1111/1468-4446.12212.Puiu, M., and C. Nistor. 2013. "Combating Fraud with Information Technologies. E-Accounting Document … A Solution?" *Network Intelligence Studies* I, no. 1, pp. 83–89.

Rodger, J.A., and J.A. George. 2017. "Triple Bottom Line Accounting for Optimizing Natural Gas Sustainability: A Statistical Linear Programming Fuzzy ILOWA Optimized Sustainment Model Approach to Reducing Supply Chain Global Cybersecurity Vulnerability through

Information and Communications Technology." *Journal of Cleaner Production* 142, pp. 1931–49. doi:10.1016/j.jclepro.2016.11.089.

Rose, J.M., B.A. McKay, C.S. Norman, and A.M. Rose. 2012. "Designing Decision Aids to Promote the Development of Expertise." *Journal of Information Systems* 26, no. 1, pp. 7–34. doi:10.2308/isys-10188.

Sanderson, I. October 2013. "Tools for IT Governance Assurance: Using Recent Updates of ISACA's Information Systems Audit and Assurance Standards alongside COBIT 5 Can Help Auditors Evaluate Their Organization's Information Systems Governance." *Internal Auditor* 70, vo. 5.

SEC v. Satyam Computer Services. April 5, 2011. "United States District Court for the District of Columbia." https://www.sec.gov/divisions/enforce/claims/docs/satyam-complaint.pdf, (accessed March 26, 2018).

Serious Fraud Office. 2018. "Tesco PLC." Filed November 4, 2014. Modified March 2, 2018. https://www.sfo.gov.uk/cases/tesco-plc/, (accessed March 26, 2018).

Silvers, J.B. June 24, 2019. "Health Care Price Transparency: Fool's Gold, or Real Money in Your Pocket?" *The Conversation*. https://theconversation.com/health-care-price-transparency-fools-gold-or-real-money-in-your-pocket-115103.

Simon, C.A., J.L. Smith, and M.F. Zimbelman. 2018. "The Influence of Judgment Decomposition on Auditors' Fraud Risk Assessments: Some Trade-Offs." *Accounting Review* 93, no. 5, 273–91. doi:10.2308/accr-52024.

Spathis, C., and J. Ananiadis. 2005. "Assessing the Benefits of Using an Enterprise System in Accounting Information and Management." *Journal of Enterprise Information Management* 18, no. 2, pp. 195–210. doi:10.1108/17410390510579918.

State of Kansas Legislative Division of Post Audit (LDPA). April 2018. "Performance Audit Report: Medicaid: Evaluating KanCare's Effect on the State's Medicaid Program." http://www.kslpa.org/media/files/reports/r-18-006.pdf, (accessed July 7, 2018).

Sy, A., and T. Tinker. 2010. "Labor Processing Labor: A New Critical Literature for Information Systems Research." *International Journal of Accounting Information Systems* 11, no. 2, pp. 120–33. doi:10.1016/j.accinf.2010.03.001.

Tan, F.T.C., Z. Guo, M. Cahalane, and D. Cheng. 2016. "Developing Business Analytic Capabilities for Combating E-commerce Identity Fraud: A Study of Trustev's Digital Verification Solution." *Information & Management* 53, no. 7, pp. 878–91. doi:10.1016/j.im.2016.07.002.

The National Archives. 2010. "Bribery Act 2010." http://www.legislation.gov.uk/ukpga/2010/23/contents, (accessed March 26, 2018).

U.S. Attorneys' Manual. 1998. "Health Care Fraud and Abuse Control Program and Guidelines." https://www.justice.gov/usam/criminal-resource-manual-978-health-care-fraud-and-abuse-control-program-and-guidelines, (accessed June 13, 2018).

U.S. Centers for Medicare and Medicaid Services (CMS). 2016. "National Health Expenditures (NHE) Fact Sheet." https://www.cms.gov/Research-Statistics-Data-and-Systems/Statistics-Trends-and-Reports/NationalHealthExpendData/NHE-Fact-Sheet.html, (accessed June 6, 2018).

U.S. Department of Health and Human Services (HHS). 2017. "Health Care Fraud and Abuse Control Annual Report for Fiscal Year 2017." https://oig.hhs.gov/publications/docs/hcfac/FY2017-hcfac.pdf, (accessed June 6, 2018).

U.S. Department of Justice Criminal Resource Manual. 1997. "Money Laundering Overview." https://www.justice.gov/usam/criminal-resource-manual-2101-money-laundering-overview, (accessed March 26, 2018).

U.S. Department of Justice. 2014. "Enron Trial Exhibits and Releases." https://www.justice.gov/archive/index-enron.html.

U.S. Department of Justice Fraud Section. 2016. "Accounting Fraud." https://www.justice.gov/criminal-fraud/sff/cases-accounting/arthrocare, (accessed March 26, 2018).

U.S. Department of Justice. December 11, 2012. "HSBC Holdings Plc. and HSBC Bank USA N.A. Admit to Anti-Money Laundering and Sanctions Violations, Forfeit $1.256 Billion in Deferred Prosecution Agreement." https://www.justice.gov/opa/pr/hsbc-holdings-plc-and-hsbc-bank-usa-na-admit-anti-money-laundering-and-sanctions-violations, (accessed March 26, 2018).

U.S. Government Accountability Office. 2009. "Federal Information System Controls Audit Manual." https://www.gao.gov/products/GAO-09-232G, (accessed June 1, 2018).

U.S. Government Accountability Office. 2014. "Standards for Internal Control in the Federal Government." https://www.gao.gov/products/GAO-14-704G, (accessed June 1, 2018).

U.S. Government Accountability Office. 2019. "Information Technology." https://www.gao.gov/assets/700/698751.pdf.

U.S. Government Accountability Office. 2010. "Organizational Transformation." https://www.gao.gov/assets/80/77233.pdf.

U.S. Office of Management and Budget (OMB). 2017. "North American Industry Classification System Manual." https://www.census.gov/eos/www/naics/2017NAICS/2017_NAICS_Manual.pdf, (accessed June 5, 2018).

U.S. Securities and Exchange Commission. 2012a. "The Securities and Exchange Commission Post-Madoff Reforms." https://www.sec.gov/spotlight/secpostmadoffreforms.htm.

U.S. Securities and Exchange Commission. 2012b. "A Resource Guide to the Foreign Corrupt Practices Act." https://www.sec.gov/spotlight/fcpa/fcpa-resource-guide.pdf, (accessed February 20, 2018).

Wall, D.S. 2018. "How Big Data Feeds Big Crime," *Global History: A Journal of Contemporary World Affairs*. https://ssrn.com/abstract=3359972.

Warren, D., and M.E. Schweitzer. 2018. "When Lying Does Not Pay: How Experts Detect Insurance Fraud." *Journal of Business Ethics* 150, no. 3, pp. 711–26.

Wildman, J.R. November 12, 1916. "Accounting a Boon to Big Business," *The New York Times*. https://nyti.ms/2F18i3v, (accessed January 24, 2018).

World Bank. 2018. "GINI Index." https://data.worldbank.org/indicator/SI.POV.GINI?locations=AF, (accessed March 25, 2018).

Wu, X. 2005. "Firm Accounting Practices, Accounting Reform and Corruption in Asia." *Policy and Society* 24, no. 3, pp. 53–78. doi:10.1016/S1449-4035(05)70060-6.

Zvezdov, D. 2012. "Rolling out Corporate Sustainability Accounting: A Set of Challenges." *Journal of Environmental Sustainability* 2, no. 2, article 3. doi: 10.14448/jes.02.0003. http://scholarworks.rit.edu/jes/vol2/iss2/3, (accessed February 7, 2018).

About the Author

David M. Shapiro serves as a distinguished lecturer and formerly deputy director of the Advanced Certificate in Forensic Accounting (MPA) program at CUNY's John Jay College of Criminal Justice, teaching fraud examination, financial forensics, and managerial inspection and oversight–related courses at the graduate and undergraduate levels presently under the Department of Public Management and formerly under the Department of Economics. He is the coordinator of the undergraduate Fraud Examination and Financial Forensics programs and deputy director of the Saturday (graduate) MPA—Inspection and Oversight program.

Among the courses taught by David are accounting information systems; advanced auditing; public sector inspection and oversight; fiscal management and capital and operational budgeting; public sector accounting and auditing; forensic accounting; public administration; advanced financial reporting; managerial accounting; financial accounting; intermediate accounting; forensic financial analysis; corporate and white-collar crime; compliance and ethics for auditors; and bureaupathology.

He has published articles in the areas of accounting, finance, and risk management. Among his published works is a special chapter for the book *How They Got Away with It: White Collar Criminals and the Financial Meltdown*. He has provided consultation in response to media inquiries from organizations such as the *New York Times*; the *Wall Street Journal*; *CBS News*, NPR, and many other outlets on topics ranging from FBI investigations to corporate fraud to Bernie Madoff to mafia crime families.

David is a financial and nonfinancial enhanced due diligence specialist. He is also an expert on financial investigations and law enforcement. His extensive background includes work as an FBI special agent and assistant legal advisor, an assistant prosecutor in Essex County, NJ, and the global practice leader at Aon's corporate investigative solutions—where he led investigations of financial crimes. He has worked as a management consultant, bankruptcy restructuring associate, independent private sector monitor/inspector general, certified public accountant, insurance claims investigator, and internal controls specialist. His former clients included Fortune 100 companies, insurance carriers, unions, governmental agencies at the federal, state, and local levels, including work under consent decrees arising from racketeering violations.

In brief, David has focused on conduct and financial crime risks, including the use of financial metrics to prevent and detect organizational and occupational frauds, such as corrupt practices and ethics violations.

Index

OTHER TITLES IN OUR FINANCIAL ACCOUNTING, AUDITING, AND TAXATION COLLECTION

Mark S. Bettner, Bucknell University; Michael P. Coyne, Fairfield University; and Roby Sawyers, *Editors*

- *Accounting Fraud, Second Edition: Maneuvering and Manipulation, Past and Present* by Gary Giroux
- *Corporate Governance in the Aftermath of the Global Financial Crisis, Volume I: Relevance and Reforms* by Zabihollah Rezaee
- *Corporate Governance in the Aftermath of the Global Financial Crisis, Volume II: Functions and Sustainability* by Zabihollah Rezaee
- *Corporate Governance in the Aftermath of the Global Financial Crisis, Volume III: Gatekeeper Functions* by Zabihollah Rezaee
- *Corporate Governance in the Aftermath of the Global Financial Crisis, Volume IV: Emerging Issues in Corporate Governance* by Zabihollah Rezaee
- *Using Accounting & Financial Information, Second Edition: Analyzing, Forecasting, and Decision Making* by Mark S. Bettner
- *Pick a Number, Second Edition: The U.S. and International Accounting* by Roger Hussey
- *The Story Underlying the Numbers: A Simple Approach to Comprehensive Financial Statements Analysis* by S. Veena Iyer
- *The Tax Aspects of Acquiring a Business, Second Edition* by W. Eugene Seago
- *Forensic Accounting and Financial Statement Fraud, Volume I: Fundamentals of Forensic Accounting* by Zabihollah Rezaee
- *Forensic Accounting and Financial Statement Fraud, Volume II: Forensic Accounting Performance* by Zabihollah Rezaee
- *A Nontechnical Guide to International Accounting* by Roger Hussey and Audra Ong

Announcing the Business Expert Press Digital Library

Concise e-books business students need for classroom and research

This book can also be purchased in an e-book collection by your library as

- *a one-time purchase,*
- *that is owned forever,*
- *allows for simultaneous readers,*
- *has no restrictions on printing, and*
- *can be downloaded as PDFs from within the library community.*

Our digital library collections are a great solution to beat the rising cost of textbooks. E-books can be loaded into their course management systems or onto students' e-book readers. The **Business Expert Press** digital libraries are very affordable, with no obligation to buy in future years. For more information, please visit **www.businessexpertpress.com/librarians**. To set up a trial in the United States, please email **sales@businessexpertpress.com**.

www.ingramcontent.com/pod-product-compliance
Lightning Source LLC
Chambersburg PA
CBHW061336220326
41599CB00026B/5205